James Opie has collected toy soldiers since he was four. From playing with them, he progressed to collecting sets as they became available. He joined the British Model Soldier Society when he was eighteen. Mr Opie has dabbled in various activities connected tenuously with toy soldiers: researching battlefield deployment, building the world's warships in 1/1200 scale, medieval wargaming in miniature, and devising boardgames. Having amassed a collection of 30,000 figures, Mr Opie became consultant valuer to Phillips, the leading auctioneers of toy soldiers. He is at present engaged in research of his favourite topic, from which books such as this are drawn.

Royal Artillery gun team in khaki Service Dress and steel helmets, with officer and four mounted gunners. At the time of writing this 1940 version, of Britains set 1339, is the most expensive set of toy soldiers ever sold at auction, costing the purchaser £8,028. Its rarity lies in the fact that Britains did not equip the figures with steel helmets until 1940, and they ceased toy soldier production in May 1941. Not more than eight sets are known to exist. (Photograph courtesy of Phillips Auctioneers, London.)

BRITISH TOY SOLDIERS
1893 TO THE PRESENT
An illustrated reference guide
for collectors

James Opie

ARMS AND ARMOUR PRESS

To inquiring collectors everywhere, particularly Peter Cowan, who discovered that BMC stands for Britannia Model Company, and whose efforts to research early British toy soldiers deserve the utmost encouragement. Also to wives and children in recognition of the fact that playing with toy soldiers sometimes seems more important to Daddy than playing with the family.

Published 1985 in Great Britain by Arms and Armour Press,
an imprint of Cassell Plc, Artillery House, Artillery Row,
London SW1P 1RT
Distributed in the United States by Sterling Publishing Co. Inc.,
2 Park Avenue, New York, N.Y. 10016.

British Library Cataloguing in Publication Data:
Opie, James
British toy soldiers, 1893 to the present day: an
illustrated reference guide for collectors.—
(Illustrated reference guides for collectors)
1. Military miniatures—Collectors and collecting
I. Title II. Series
745.592'82 NK8475.M5
ISBN 0-85368-959-8

Designed by David Gibbons. Edited by Michael Boxall.
Typeset by Typesetters (Birmingham) Limited.
Printed and bound in Great Britain
by Biddles Ltd., Guildford & Kings Lynn.

CONTENTS

INTRODUCTION

In 1970 a little book by L. W. Richards was published, entitled *Old British Model Soldiers, 1893–1918*. It simply contained sixty pages of pictures of toy soldiers, with a brief commentary, but because Len Richards, who, sadly, died in 1980, was the pioneer of systematic collecting, the book has until now remained the most useful illustrated guide available. Both editions are long out of print, and it has been my privilege to be asked by the publishers to provide a replacement work.

Toy soldier collecting has evolved somewhat since that original volume appeared. No longer, for instance, are collectors ashamed to call their collections toys rather than models. Nowadays, the making, painting and collecting of military miniatures is a more sharply differentiated branch of the hobby, and the collecting, restoration and conversion of toy soldiers has grown in status and has become a well-defined pastime of its own. Both hobbies, however, are still catered for by the same British Model Soldier Society which Len Richards served so well as President and Honorary Treasurer. In 1985, the Society celebrated its Golden Jubilee.

In a new book, new opportunities arise. Since this book replaces the previous one, a proportion of the important early figures are shown again, but this time examples of British-made toy figures right up to the 1984 issues are included. Where appropriate, figures illustrated in the previous book have been shown from a different angle. Although a large part of the pleasure of collecting is to be able to show off whole regiments of the same figure marching together, in this book, just one example of each is shown.

The history of toy soldier manufacture in Great Britain started in 1893, when William Britain and his family invented the hollow-cast method of production. From then until the late 1950s, the majority of toy soldiers were made by this method, which results in a hollow lead alloy model. Most figures were about 2⅛ inches, or 54mm tall, this being the scale on which Britains standardized, and which is now known as the standard or 54mm scale. After the first British plastic toy soldiers were manufactured in 1947, it took until about 1960 for them to become the normal type on offer in the shops. Britains stopped hollow-cast production in 1966, and since then plastic has reigned supreme. Since 1972, the interest in collecting has been so great that new, solid metal figures, reproducing the style of the old hollow metal ones, have been put on the market specifically for collectors of toy soldiers. Britains Ltd itself has participated in this trend, and developed a new metal diecasting technique to produce sets for the souvenir and collector market.

Britains Ltd has always been the leader in British-made toy soldiers, and so more than one-third of the figures illustrated are by this company. Other firms, with the approximate dates during which they were operating, are given in the index of manufacturers on page 72. Nearly all the figures shown were made in Great Britain for the commercial toy market, the exception being those made for the collector market from

1973 to the present, and a few imported from Hong Kong by British manufacturers or importers.

The description of each figure has been kept minimal in order to leave more space for the photographs. Information given is usually limited to the manufacturer (where known), the *approximate* first year of manufacture (remembering that some models were manufactured during periods of many years) and any note of particular importance or interest, such as the regimental title or set number. (Many manufacturers changed their set or reference numbers frequently, as their price lists were revised, so a lot of these numbers have yet to be determined.) All figures are hollow-cast except those designated (S) solid-cast, (P) plastic, (A) Aluminium and (D) die-cast metal. All figures are 54mm scale except where the scale is given in brackets e.g. (60mm) or (35mm). The relative size of the various scales is apparent from the photographs, since all the figures in each plate have been photographed together.

As in the original volume, the figures are organized by subject, and the majority were produced after 1918. I have included not only rare types, but also many of those likely to be found in jumble sales or collectors' 'swop-meets'. I have taken a strict view of toy soldiers as being military types, and thus cowboys and indians, pirates, spacemen, Boy Scouts, civilians and animals have all been excluded except for some police and native warriors. Apart from the odd cannon, separately manufactured military equipment has also been omitted, as have the unpainted toy soldiers produced by plastic kit manufacturers such as Airfix or Matchbox. With space to show only 1,110 examples, this is by no means a definitive display, but I hope that the variety shown will be sufficient to whet the appetite and provide a glimpse of the vast diversity available.

SELECT BIBLIOGRAPHY

The following books contain further information about British-made toy soldiers:

CARMAN, W. Y. *Model Soldiers.* Charles Letts & Co., 1972
GARDINER, G. AND MORRIS, A. *All-Colour Directory of Metal Toys.* Salamander, 1984
GARRATT, JOHN G. *Model Soldiers, a Collector's Guide.* Seeley Service, 1965
— (Ed.). World Encyclopaedia of Model Soldiers. Muller, 1981
JOHNSON, PETER. *Toy Armies.* Batsford, 1982
MCKENZIE, IAN. *Collecting Old Toy Soldiers.* Batsford, 1975
OPIE, JAMES. *Britains Toy Soldiers*, 1893–1932. Gollancz, 1985
—On Guard Toy Soldier Exhibition Catalogue. New Cavendish, 1984
—*Toy Soldiers.* Shire Publications, 1983
RICHARDS, L. W. *Old British Model Soldiers*, 1893–1918. Arms & Armour Press, 1970
RUDDELL, JOANNE AND RON. *The Britains Collector's Checklist.* Private publication
RUDDLE, JOHN. *Collector's Guide to Britains Model Soldiers.* Model & Allied Publications, 1980
WALLIS, JOE. *Regiments of All Nations.* Private publication, 1981

Private publications, reprinted catalogues, periodicals and other useful literature can often be obtained from dealers or at meetings of the British Model Soldier Society (Secretary: David Pearce, 22 Lynwood Road, Ealing, London W5 1JJ). Back numbers of the catalogues of toy soldier auctions, together with the prices realized, may be purchased from Phillips Auctioneers. That of the Richards Collection is the most useful and contains ninety-nine photographs.

PRICE GUIDE FOR 1988/89

The Price guide is in two parts. Part I gives the current price of the figure shown (all figures are assumed to be complete and in good condition). Part II gives the set contents where the set is referred to in the text, with the price of a complete set in good condition in its manufacturer's original box.

The price given is that for which the figure or set might well be available if found at auction or through a dealer. There is, however, no reason why any two people negotiating a price have to stay anywhere near these prices; they are merely my personal estimate of the likely price at the time of writing, using my knowledge of the rarity and desirability of the figures illustrated. The price goes up if many collectors want something and there are few available (rarity) and goes down if because of an item's ugliness or frailty, few collectors want it (desirability). Other factors may also enter into the negotiation: availability, the chance of seeing another one quickly at a cheaper price; condition, the price falling steeply with the amount of paint knocked off, and even more steeply with breakages. On the other hand, some figures are so rare that only broken examples may be available. Complete sets and original boxes also make a big difference, as can be seen from a multiplication of the prices in Part I against the prices in Part II. Above all, if a collector finds a figure that is particularly interesting to him he may be prepared to pay double or more what anyone else would consider to be a fair price. Dealers or auctioneers with large stocks for sale specialize in satisfying the demands of these more discriminating collectors, and so can sometimes command prices well in excess of those given here. Prices at auction in particular are often affected by changes in the international currency exchange rates when many foreign bidders are present.

Here is an example of the sort of difference made to prices by the condition of an item. Plate 15 figure 10 is a very rare Britains 'plug shouldered' Scots Grey. A mint boxed set of six of these in original paint might well be worth £5,000. If one were broken, the price would be about £3,500. If the box were in poor condition, £3,000. If in good condition but without box, £2,500. If one figure were missing, £2,000. If both box and figures were in poor condition, £1,000. The single figure in excellent condition without a box is worth about £150. If a tail were missing, £30. If paintwork were poor, £25. If repainted (as shown in Plate 15) £20. If the plug arm were missing, £10. While there is nearly always a residual value in any toy soldier, as can be seen from the above, the mint boxed price may well be a very different affair from the poor condition or damaged price, and ascertaining the condition is essential before any negotiation can take place.

PRICE GUIDE TO INDIVIDUAL ITEMS SHOWN.

An asterisk (*) against the price means that the figure shown is not complete or in good enough condition to merit the 'complete and in good condition' price quoted. A □ against the price means that a set content and price is quoted in the set price section.

PLATE 1
1 £2.00
2 £3.00□
3 30p□
4 £1.00
5 £2.00
6 £3.00□
7 £1.00
8 £1.50
9 £10.00
10 £1.00□
11 £2.00
12 £8.00□
13 £6.00□
14 £60.00□
15 50p□
16 £4.00□
17 £3.00
18 £3.00
19 £130.00□
20 £5.00

PLATE 2
1 £25.00□
2 £18.00
3 £12.00□
4 £7.00□
5 £6.00*□
6 £7.00□
7 £8.00□
8 £9.00□
9 £1.50*□
10 50p□
11 £1.50□
12 £1.00□

PLATE 3
1 £100.00□
2 £30.00□
3 £12.00□
4 £12.00□
5 £25.00□
6 £40.00□
7 £18.00□
8 £25.00□
9 £30.00□
10 £30.00□
11 £8.00*
12 £6.00*

PLATE 4
1 £2.00
2 £10.00
3 £3.00
4 £10.00□
5 £12.00□
6 £3.00
7 £2.00□
8 £4.00
9 £10.00*
10 £2.00
11 £5.00
12 £6.00

PLATE 5
1 £1.50
2 £3.00□
3 £2.50
4 £2.50
5 £2.00
6 £1.50
7 £20.00□
8 £6.00□
9 40p□
10 40p□
11 20p*
12 10p
13 40p
14 £1.00
15 £1.00
16 £2.50
17 £1.25□
18 75p
19 £1.00
20 £1.50□
21 80p□
22 £1.00*
23 40p

PLATE 6
1 30p□
2 £8.00□
3 £8.00□
4 £10.00□
5 £12.00□
6 £1.50
7 £1.25□
8 50p□
9 £3.00
10 £1.50
11 £1.00
12 75p
13 £1.00
14 50p
15 50p
16 £1.50
17 40p
18 35p
19 £2.00
20 £3.00
21 40p
22 40p
23 £3.50
24 £3.50

PLATE 7
1 £7.00□
2 £5.50
3 £5.00
4 £25.00□
5 £8.00
6 £1.50□
7 £2.50
8 £1.00
9 £4.00*□
10 £2.50*
11 £2.50

12 £2.00*
13 £3.00
14 £1.50
15 £3.00
16 75p*
17 £2.00
18 £25.00□
19 £25.00□
20 £4.00
21 £2.00
22 £2.00
23 £2.00
24 £1.00

PLATE 8
1 £30.00□
2 £12.00□
3 £18.00□
4 £50.00□
5 £2.00
6 £1.50
7 £1.25
8 £1.50
9 £2.00□
10 £2.50□
11 £2.00□
12 £2.00□
13 £1.50□
14 50p
15 £2.50□
16 £3.00□
17 40p
18 60p
19 50p*
20 50p*
21 30p
22 75p*
23 40p
24 40p

PLATE 9
1 £1.50
2 £2.00
3 60p
4 £2.50
5 £2.00
6 £2.00
7 £3.00*
8 £4.00□
9 £1.00
10 £1.00
11 £1.00
12 £1.00
13 £2.00
14 60p
15 50p
16 80p
17 £3.00□
18 £2.50□
19 2.50□
20 £3.00□
21 £2.00□
22 50p

23 50p
24 £1.00

PLATE 10
1 £2.00
2 £12.00□
3 £18.00□
4 £8.00□
5 £5.00□
6 £12.00□
7 £1.50*□
8 £1.50
9 £1.00
10 £1.00
11 30p
12 15p
13 £1.50
14 60p
15 £3.00
16 50p
17 £10.00□
18 £9.00□
19 £8.00□
20 £7.00□
21 £7.00□
22 £1.50
23 £2.00□
24 £2.50□

PLATE 11
1 £20.00*□
2 £20.00□
3 £20.00□
4 £30.00□
5 £7.00□
6 80p
7 £2.00□
8 40p
9 40p
10 40p□
11 20p
12 20p
13 £5.00
14 £1.50
15 60p
16 £1.50*□
17 30p
18 20p
19 20p

PLATE 12
1 £60.00□
2 £8.00□
3 £4.00□
4 £10.00□
5 £5.00
6 £3.00□
7 £2.00□
8 £2.00□
9 £1.25
10 75p
11 75p
12 75p

13 £5.00
14 40p
15 30p
16 30p
17 50p
18 30p*
19 60p*
20 50p
21 50p
22 £2.50□
23 £2.50□
24 £2.00□

PLATE 13
1 £1.00
2 £1.00
3 £22.00□
4 £8.00□
5 £7.00□
6 £5.50□
7 £1.50
8 60p
9 80p
10 50p
11 40p□
12 40p□
13 20p
14 20p
15 20p
16 80p
17 50p*
18 £3.50□
19 £3.50□
20 £3.00□
21 £4.00□
22 £1.50
23 £1.50

PLATE 14
1 £5.00
2 £25.00
3 £7.00□
4 £30.00□
5 £4.00□
6 £1.50
7 £15.00*
8 £20.00
9 £1.25
10 £3.00
11 £2.00□
12 £2.50

PLATE 15
1 £1.50*
2 £8.00*□
3 £4.00
4 £1.00
5 £18.00□
6 £16.00□
7 £5.00□
8 £12.00*□
9 £30.00□
10 £200.00*□

11 £15.00□
12 £15.00□
13 £2.50

PLATE 16
1 £50.00□
2 £35.00□
3 £25.00□
4 £20.00□
5 £40.00□
6 £30.00□
7 £2.00
8 £12.00□
9 £35.00□
10 £8.00□
11 £8.00□
12 £3.00
13 £2.00
14 £10.00□

PLATE 17
1 £8.00
2 £8.00
3 £4.00
4 £6.00
5 £3.00
6 £10.00
7 £2.50
8 £3.00
9 £1.50
10 £1.25
11 £4.00
12 £2.00

PLATE 18
1 £40.00□
2 £15.00*
3 £10.00
4 £4.00
5 £20.00□
6 £25.00□
7 £20.00*□
8 £4.00
9 £16.00□
10 £16.00□
11 £25.00□
12 £25.00*□

PLATE 19
1 £20.00□
2 £15.00□
3 £3.00□
4 £40.00
5 £2.50
6 £2.00
7 £3.50
8 £2.50□
9 £2.00
10 £10.00
11 £18.00
12 £2.50
13 £2.50

PLATE 20
1 £10.00
2 £3.00
3 £3.00
4 £4.00
5 £8.00
6 £5.00
7 £15.00
8 £20.00
9 £50.00
10 £25.00
11 £10.00
12 £5.00
13 £25.00
14 50p
15 £1.25
16 75p
17 £5.00
18 £4.00
19 £3.00
20 £1.00
21 £8.00
22 £1.00

PLATE 21
1 £3.00
2 £1.50
3 75p
4 50p
5 75p
6 75p
7 £1.00
8 30p
9 £3.00
10 £1.50
11 £2.00
12 £1.50
13 £1.00
14 £4.00
15 £8.00
16 £10.00
17 £15.00
18 £60.00
19 £4.00
20 £2.00
21 £2.00
22 £2.50
23 £2.50

PLATE 22
1 £8.00
2 £5.00
3 £12.00
4 £75.00
5 £4.00
6 £6.00
7 £6.00
8 £1.50*
9 £4.00*
10 50p*
11 60p*
12 £2.50
13 £2.00
14 £2.00
15 £3.00*
16 £1.25
17 £3.00*
18 £3.00*
19 £3.00
20 £2.00
21 £1.00*

22 75p
23 £2.00
24 £1.50

PLATE 23
1 £7.00
2 £4.00
3 £8.00*
4 £6.00*
5 £1.50
6 £3.00
7 10p
8 £1.50
9 £4.00
10 £4.00
11 £1.00
12 £2.50
13 £5.00
14 £5.00
15 £5.00
16 £4.50
17 £2.50
18 £3.00
19 50p
20 £2.50
21 40p
22 40p
23 £2.00
24 £1.50

PLATE 24
1 £4.50
2 £4.50
3 £4.50
4 £4.50
5 £2.00
6 £2.00*
7 £6.00
8 £2.50
9 £3.00
10 £1.50
11 £1.00
12 £3.00
13 £3.00
14 £3.00
15 £6.00
16 £30.00
17 £60.00
18 £3.00
19 £3.00
20 £3.00
21 £3.00
22 £3.00
23 £3.00
24 £3.00
25 £3.00

PLATE 25
1 £15.00
2 £250.00*
3 £30.00
4 £25.00*
5 £8.00
6 £2.50
7 £3.00
8 £8.00
9 £25.00
10 £15.00
11 £12.00
12 £20.00
13 £8.00

14 £5.00

PLATE 26
1 £25.00
2 £15.00*
3 £50.00
4 £12.00
5 £12.00
6 £6.00
7 £20.00
8 £10.00
9 £45.00
10 £35.00
11 £3.00
12 £10.00*
13 £6.00
14 £5.00
15 £10.00*
16 £50.00
17 £50.00
18 £50.00
19 £30.00
20 £75.00

PLATE 27
1 £30.00*
2 £25.00
3 £40.00
4 £45.00
5 £60.00
6 £30.00
7 £8.00
8 £2.00
9 £2.00
10 £5.00
11 £1.50
12 £1.50
13 £1.50
14 50p
15 £6.00
16 £3.00
17 £7.00
18 £1.50
19 £14.00
20 £1.50
21 £1.50

PLATE 28
1 £75.00
2 £5.00
3 £20.00
4 £20.00
5 £4.00
6 £3.00
7 £5.00
8 £8.00
9 £20.00*
10 £18.00
11 £2.00
12 £3.00*
13 £6.00
14 £8.00
15 £2.00*
16 £1.00
17 £12.00
18 £7.00
19 £12.00
20 £3.00
21 75p
22 £4.00
23 £5.00

24 £3.00

PLATE 29
1 £15.00
2 £10.00
3 £6.00*
4 £40.00*
5 £60.00
6 £6.00
7 £10.00
8 £8.00
9 £40.00
10 £12.00
11 £40.00
12 £10.00
13 £20.00
14 £5.00
15 £2.50
16 £1.00
17 £4.00
18 £60.00
19 £5.00
20 £10.00
21 £8.00*
22 £6.00
23 £2.00
24 £4.00*

PLATE 30
1 £25.00
2 £25.00
3 £12.00
4 £75.00
5 £25.00
6 £20.00
7 £5.00
8 £3.00
9 80p
10 £4.00
11 £35.00
12 £8.00
13 £3.50
14 £2.50
15 £8.00
16 £5.00
17 £10.00
18 £9.00
19 £5.00
20 £3.00
21 £20.00

PLATE 31
1 £2.00
2 £8.00
3 £5.00
4 £4.00
5 £8.00
6 £2.50
7 £2.00
8 £2.00
9 £2.00
10 £5.00
11 £3.00
12 £2.00
13 £5.00
14 £3.00
15 £15.00
16 £12.00
17 £12.00
18 £1.00
19 £1.00

20 50p
21 £1.00
22 £1.00
23 £1.00
24 75p
25 50p
26 £1.00
27 £1.50
28 £8.00

PLATE 32
1 £15.00
2 £6.00
3 £15.00
4 £8.00
5 £8.00
6 £10.00
7 £3.00
8 £10.00
9 £2.00
10 £10.00
11 £5.00
12 £3.00
13 £6.00
14 £3.00
15 £2.50
16 £1.50
17 £2.00
18 £1.50
19 £1.00
20 £1.00
21 £3.00
22 £2.00
23 £10.00

PLATE 33
1 £15.00
2 £6.00
3 £1.50
4 £2.00
5 £4.00
6 £1.50
7 £1.00
8 75p
9 £1.00
10 £2.00
11 £2.50
12 £3.00
13 £5.00
14 £4.00
15 £5.00
16 £3.00
17 £15.00
18 £2.50
19 £15.00

PLATE 34
1 £6.00
2 £60.00
3 £15.00
4 £2.50
5 £1.00
6 £1.50
7 £6.00
8 £30.00
9 £6.00
10 50p
11 30p
12 50p
13 £1.50
14 60p

15 75p
16 £1.50
17 £2.00
18 £2.50
19 50p*
20 75p
21 £1.50
22 60p
23 £12.00
24 £7.00

PLATE 35
1 £1.50
2 £2.50
3 60p
4 75p
5 60p
6 £1.00
7 50p
8 £40.00
9 £3.00
10 £1.50
11 £1.50
12 £1.00
13 50p
14 60p
15 50p
16 30p
17 30p
18 50p
19 40p
20 40p
21 50p
22 40p
23 50p
24 40p

PLATE 36
1 £1.00
2 £2.50
3 £1.00
4 £1.50
5 40p
6 50p
7 25p
8 25p
9 £1.50
10 60p
11 £1.00
12 £1.50
13 £2.50
14 £1.00
15 £1.00
16 £1.00
17 £1.00
18 £1.50
19 £2.50
20 £1.50
21 50p
22 50p
23 50p
24 50p
25 50p
26 £6.00

PLATE 37
1 50p
2 20p
3 50p
4 50p
5 50p

6 50p	**PLATE 40**	5 £7.00	9 £3.50	14 £16.00	19 £3.00*
7 50p	1 £7.00	6 £5.00	10 £1.00	15 £30.00	
8 50p	2 £5.00	7 £10.00	11 £8.00	16 £16.00	**PLATE 53**
9 30p	3 £15.00	8 £3.00	12 £1.20	17 £2.00	1 50p
10 £1.20	4 £15.00	9 £2.00	13 £2.00	18 £3.00	2 £1.20
11 £1.20	5 £20.00	10 £8.00	14 £15.00	19 £18.00	3 £1.50
12 £1.20	6 £13.00	11 £3.00	15 £3.00		4 60p
13 30p	7 £12.00	12 £1.20	16 £15.00*	**PLATE 50**	5 30p
14 30p	8 £15.00	13 £20.00	17 £8.00	1 £2.50	6 50p
15 50p*	9 £15.00	14 £7.00	18 £12.00	2 £1.20	7 50p
16 50p*	10 £8.00	15 £2.50		3 £1.50	8 £3.00*
17 £1.50	11 £7.00	16 £1.50	**PLATE 47**	4 £2.50	9 £2.00*
18 £2.00	12 £40.00	17 £2.50	1 £4.00	5 £2.00	10 50p
19 £1.00	13 £12.00	18 £3.50	2 £1.00	6 £1.50	11 50p
20 20p	14 £2.50		3 75p	7 £1.50	12 £1.20
21 20p	15 £2.50	**PLATE 44**	4 £6.00	8 75p	13 £1.50
22 20p	16 £1.50	1 £25.00	5 £7.00	9 £2.00	14 £8.00
23 £1.50	17 80p	2 £10.00	6 50p	10 60p	15 £12.00
	18 £1.20	3 £20.00	7 £6.00	11 £1.50	16 £4.00
PLATE 38	19 £1.50	4 £3.00	8 £12.00	12 £1.50	17 £4.00*
1 £8.00	20 £1.20	5 £8.00	9 £8.00	13 £1.50	18 £6.00
2 £6.00	21 £6.00	6 £16.00	10 £1.00	14 £1.50	19 £2.00
3 £12.00	22 £2.00	7 £10.00*	11 £1.50	15 60p	
4 £7.00	23 £1.00	8 £10.00	12 50p	16 £2.00	**PLATE 54**
5 £8.00		9 £10.00	13 50p	17 £1.50	1 30p
6 £2.50	**PLATE 41**	10 £4.00	14 50p	18 £10.00	2 £2.00
7 £8.00	1 £3.00	11 £5.00	15 £1.50	19 £1.50	3 £1.50
8 £10.00	2 £1.00	12 £10.00	16 £4.00	20 £1.25	4 £3.50
9 £8.00*	3 £1.00	13 £14.00	17 £2.00	21 40p	5 £1.75
10 £8.00	4 £3.50	14 £10.00	18 £3.00	22 £1.50	6 £1.00
11 £2.00	5 £5.00	15 £50.00	19 £20.00	23 75p	7 £3.00
12 £2.00	6 £6.00*	16 £50.00*		24 £5.00	8 £1.20
13 £1.50	7 £12.00	17 £20.00	**PLATE 48**		9 £1.00
14 £1.00	8 £18.00	18 £5.00	1 £100	**PLATE 51**	10 75p*
15 50p	9 £40.00	19 £25.00	2 £20.00	1 £9.00	11 75p*
16 60p	10 £25.00	20 £25.00	3 £25.00	2 £6.00	12 75p
17 £1.50	11 £10.00	21 £9.00	4 £12.00	3 £12.00	13 75p
18 75p	12 £12.00*	22 £75.00	5 £25.00	4 £5.00	14 £3.00
19 75p	13 £15.00		6 £20.00	5 £7.00	15 £3.50
20 £1.50	14 £6.00	**PLATE 45**	7 £25.00	6 £6.00	16 £5.00
21 £1.00	15 £40.00	1 £5.00	8 £15.00	7 £1.50	17 £1.00
22 £1.20	16 £40.00	2 £12.00	9 £6.00	8 75p	18 £1.00
23 £1.00	17 £10.00	3 £15.00	10 £40.00	9 £1.00	19 £1.00
24 £1.50		4 £18.00	11 £8.00	10 50p	20 £1.00
	PLATE 42	5 £8.00	12 £3.00	11 40p	
PLATE 39	1 £7.00	6 £30.00	13 £8.00	12 30p	**PLATE 55**
1 £30.00	2 £45.00	7 £20.00	14 £4.00	13 £12.00	1 £1.00
2 £15.00	3 £40.00	8 £15.00	15 £20.00	14 £2.00	2 £1.00
3 £13.00	4 £10.00	9 £8.00	16 £15.00	15 50p	3 £1.50
4 £10.00	5 £60.00	10 £7.00	17 £8.00	15 50p	4 £1.50
5 £8.00	6 £40.00	11 £7.00	18 £7.00		5 £5.00
6 £12.00	7 £7.00*	12 £5.00	19 £6.00	**PLATE 52**	6 £3.00*
7 £4.00	8 £5.00	13 £35.00	20 £12.00	1 £3.00	7 £1.20
8 £3.00	9 £2.50	14 £6.00	21 £25.00	2 £3.00	8 £15.00
9 £2.50	10 £7.00	15 £25.00	22 £100.00	3 £1.50	9 £15.00
10 £2.50	11 £4.00*	16 £20.00		4 £2.00	10 £20.00
11 £1.50	12 £30.00*	17 £5.00	**PLATE 49**	5 £3.00	11 £15.00
12 £1.20	13 £25.00*	18 £18.00	1 £10.00	6 £3.00	12 £1.20
13 £7.00	14 £35.00*	19 £35.00	2 £9.00	7 £1.20	13 £7.00
14 £5.00	15 £10.00*	20 £10.00	3 £4.00	8 £1.00	14 £2.50
15 £2.50	16 £7.00		4 £3.00	9 £1.50	15 £10.00
16 £4.00	17 £15.00	**PLATE 46**	5 £2.50	10 £1.00	16 75p
17 £4.50	18 £15.00	1 £10.00	6 £2.50	11 £1.20	17 75p
18 £4.50	19 £15.00	2 £4.00	7 £2.50	12 60p	18 £1.50
19 £3.50		3 £1.00	8 £12.00	13 £1.00	19 75p
20 £4.50	**PLATE 43**	4 £3.00	9 £7.00	14 75p	
21 £5.00	1 £10.00	5 £8.00	10 £12.00	15 25p	
22 £5.00	2 £15.00	6 £8.00	11 £9.00	16 £10.00	
23 £5.00	3 £12.00	7 £2.50	12 £9.00	17 £2.50	
24 £15.00	4 £20.00	8 £2.50	13 £16.00	18 £4.00*	

PRICE GUIDE TO SETS

These prices are those applicable to excellent figures correctly contained in excellent boxes.

PLATE 1
2: Complete coach and eighteen attendants £200
3: Nineteen attendants £15
6: Five men and one with lantern £30
10: Two yeomen, five Life Guards £15
12: Eighteen attendants £120
13: Eight Yeomen with captain £100
14: Eight gentlemen with captain £800
15: Two each of three souvenir figures £4
16: Six different souvenir figures £30
19: Singly boxed £30
PLATE 2
1: Officer and four troopers £300
2: Officer and four troopers £200
3: Officer and four troopers £100
4: Officer and four troopers £90
5: Officer and four troopers £80
6: Officer and four assorted troopers £80
7 and **8:** Officer and four assorted troopers £90
9: Assorted three mounted, three on foot £20
10: One mounted, six on foot and sentry box £5
11: Officer and six troopers £25
12: Individually boxed £1.75
PLATE 3
1: Officer and five men with special heads, officer and five men with normal heads £3,000
2: As **Plate 2:** 3
3: As **Plate 2:** 4
4: As **Plate 2:** 6
5: Large display set, Horse Guards and Coldstream Guards, 71 pieces, £8,000
6: Twelve musicians £2,000
7: Twelve musicians £250
8: Four trumpeters, kettledrummer and eighteen troopers with lances £800
9: Standard and six assorted escort £250
10: Individually boxed £25
PLATE 4
4: Trumpeter and four troopers £120
5: Officer and four troopers with swords £110
7: Four troopers £20
PLATE 5
2: Six troopers £50
7: Individually boxed £25
8: Four on foot and two mounted £90
9: Seven assorted on foot £15
10: Two each of three souvenir figures £4
17: Six on foot and one mounted £20
20: Four on foot and two mounted £25
21: Six on foot and one mounted £15
PLATE 6
1: Eight figures £15
2: Six figures, piper and officer £200
3: Seven figures and officer £150
4: Officer and seven men £150
5: Three sergeants, two Colours and two officers £300
7: Officer and five men £20
8: Sergeant and five men £8

PLATE 7
1: Seven pipers £90
2: Seven pipers £70
3: Seven pipers £60
4 and **5:** Officers, piper and two men £200
6: Standard-bearer and six marching men £30
18 and **19: As Plate 6:** 5
PLATE 8
1–4: Twenty-one musicians £1500
9–13 + 15 and **16:** Standard-bearer and thirteen musicians £80
PLATE 9
8: Twenty-one musicians £120
17–21: Twenty musicians £80
PLATE 10
2: As **Plate 6:** 2
3: As **Plate 6:** 2
4: Colour-bearer and seven pioneers £150
5: Officer, piper and six marching men £90
6: As **Plate 6:** 5
7: As **Plate 6:** 7
17: Display set of 118 assorted £6,000
18: Six with mounted officer £180
19: Display set of 118 assorted £6,000
20 and **21:** Sentry with box £25
23: Eleven assorted £40
24: As **Plate 7:** 6
PLATE 11:
1: Display set of Coldstream Guards and Horse Guards, 71 pieces £8,000
2: Display set of Grenadier Guards and East Kent Regiment, nineteen pieces £400
3: As **Plate 11:** 2
4: As **Plate 10:** 18
5: Officer and seven men £100
7: Officer and six men £30
10: Four assorted on a card £5
12: Six assorted £1
PLATE 12
1: As **Plate 10:** 17
2–5: Thirty assorted £400
6 and **7:** Thirty assorted £250
8: Eight assorted £70
22–24: Eight assorted £35
PLATE 13
3: Officer and six running men £150
4–6: As **Plate 10:** 17
11 and **12:** Five assorted £4
18 and **19:** Drummer and five marching men £35
20 and **21:** Officer and seven marching men £60
PLATE 14
2: Officer and four troopers £350
4: Officer and four troopers £300
5: Officer and five troopers £40
11: Five troopers £25
PLATE 15
2: Officer and three troopers £90
5: Officer and four troopers £350
6: Officer and four troopers £320
7: Officer and four troopers £80
8: Individually boxed £30

9: Officer mounted and two dismounted troopers £250
10: Officer, trumpeter and four troopers £5,000
PLATE 16
1 and 2: Officer and four troopers £400
3 and 4: Officer and four troopers £200
5: Officer and four assorted troopers £800
6: Officer and four troopers £400
8: Officer and four troopers £200
9: Officer and four troopers £400
10 and 11: Officer, three troopers and four horses £200
14: Officer and four assorted troopers £110
PLATE 18
1: Officer, trumpeter and seven troopers £2500
4: Five troopers £35
5 and 6: Trumpeter and four troopers £350
7: Officer and four troopers £130
9: Officer and four troopers £200
10: Officer and four troopers £150
11 and 12: Officer and four troopers £400
PLATE 19
1 and 2: Officer and four troopers £200
3: Officer and five troopers £30
8: Five troopers £30
PLATE 20
2: Eight charging £80
3: Eight charging £70
4: Eight charging £80
7 and 8: Officer and four running men, with two pipers £400
9 and 10: One mounted and four on foot £250
11: Eight marching men £200
12: Seven marching men with piper £80
13: Two standard-bearers, four sergeants £600
14: Officer and six marching men £20
15: Officer and five men £6
PLATE 21
2: Seven men £20
9 and 10: Officer, piper and nine men £80
15: Piper and four marching men £80
16: Eight marching men £150
17: Eight marching men £200
18: Officer and six marching men £900
PLATE 22
1: Ten assorted £100
2: Ten assorted £90
3: Individually boxed £20
4: Officer and nine men lying firing £250
5: As **Plate 22:** 1
6 and 7: As **Plate 22:** 4
10: Eight men £15
11: Eight men £15
12 and 13: Officer and five men £15
22: Seven men £20
PLATE 23
3: As **Plate 20:** 7
4: As **Plate 20:** 12
5: Seven pipers £20
19: Six musicians £15
PLATE 24:
1-3: Eight figures, assorted arms £90

4: Eight figures, assorted arms £100
5: Nine figures £25
4: Eight figures, assorted arms £100
5: Nine figures £25
8: Six figures £20
9: Six figures, assorted £30
16: Trumpeter and four troopers £300
17: Mounted officer, nine assorted running men, gun, two gunners and tip-up board £5,000
PLATE 25
1: Six figures £300
2: Large display box with 275 figures £20,000
3 and 4: Trumpeter and four troopers £250
9: Four troopers and officer £250
10: Four troopers and officer £120
11: Eight men £250
12: Eight men £400
PLATE 26
1: Five figures £300
3: Officer and four men £600
4: Officer and two men £80
5: Officer and nine men on guard £150
6: Ten men firing £120
7: Eight marching men £600
8: Eight marching men £120
9: Two wagons, mounted officer and ten men £6,500
10: Officer and seven men £600
11: Officer and five men £25
13: Eight marching men £120
14: Eight marching men £80
15: Eight marching men £200
16: Eight marching men £600
17 and 20: Officer and seven men £1000
18: Eight men £1000
19: Officer and seven men £800
PLATE 27
1: Gun team with limber, gun, four seated gunners and officer £3,000
2: Gun team with limber, gun, four mounted gunners and officer £1000
3: Gun team with limber, gun, four seated gunners and officer £1,200
4: Gun team with limber, gun, four seated gunners and officer £1,500
5: Gun team with limber, gun and officer £3,500
6: Officer, gun and six gunners £130
7: Officer with seven assorted gunners £80
8: Individually boxed £4
15: Spotter and chair £15
PLATE 28
1: Four figures and ammunition £1000
3 and 4, 9 and **10, 22:** Display set of 41 figures £3,000
6 and 20: Five kneeling, five standing men £40
7: Officer, drummer, four men kneeling, four men standing £150
8: Eight figures £200
17:: Officer and seven men £180
18 and 19: Officer and nine men £130
24: Four musicians £15
PLATE 29
1: Officer and seven men £300

2: Officer and seven men running £150
5: Seven assorted officers £1,500
9: Officer and seven men £1,200
10: Officer and seven men £150
12: Officer and seven mon £120
13 and **14:** Officer, two men and goat £200
18: Mounted officer and eight men £4,500
19: Officer, six men and goat £90
20: Officer, seven men and goat £250
21: Officer and six men £90
22: Officer and six men £90
PLATE 30
1 and **6:** Two officers and two aides-de-camp £150
2 and **3:** Three assorted officers, horse and dispatch rider £200
4: As **Plate 29:** 5
5: Two officers and two aides-de-camp £150
11: Twenty assorted railwaymen, passengers and luggage £300
12-20: Twenty-four assorted £250
21: Motor ambulance and seventeen assorted £300
PLATE 31: 2–6: Eight medical figures £100
PLATE 32
1: Mounted officer and six men £150
2 and **3:** Officer and seven men £100
4 and **5:** Four of each £100
6: Four men with guns £60
10: Twenty-four assorted £150
11: Eight men £70
12: Officer and seven men £60
13: Officer and six men £70
PLATE 33
13: Fourteen assorted £300
14: Officer and seven men £70
19: Four dispatch-riders £100
PLATE 34
1: Eight men £80
2: Eight men £700
3: Officer and seven men £150
4: Officer and seven assorted £45
8: One detector, two stretcher-parties £250
23 and **24:** Sentry box £30
PLATE 35
1 and **2:** Nine assorted £30
7: Eight assorted £15
8: Officer and seven men £900
9: Officer and seven men £70
15: Eight assorted £15
23 and **24:** Five assorted £8
PLATE 36
1: Seven assorted £6
4: Ten assorted £35
11: Nine assorted £20
PLATE 37
1 and **3–8:** Eight as shown £15
PLATE 38
1 and **2:** Petty Officer and seven ratings £120
1 and **3:** Petty Officer and seven ratings £180
1 and **4:** Petty Officer, eight ratings, limber and gun £250
7 and **8:** Eight assorted £100

24: Eight assorted £15
PLATE 39
1: Officer and seven men £500
2 and **3:** Officer and seven men £150
4: Officer and seven men £120
5: Officer and seven men £100
6: Seven Officers assorted £120
7: Eight ratings £60
8: 13 musicians £50
13: Officer and seven men £100
14: Officer and seven men £80
15: Officer and five men £25
16: Thirty musicians £150
PLATE 40
1: Two Officers and six airmen £120
2, 5, 7 and **9:** Twenty-two assorted £400
3: Twenty-one musicians £800
4: Twelve musicians £300
6 and **8:** Two WAAF and six pilots £200
10 and **11:** Officer and seven airmen £100
12: Officer, colour-bearer and two sergeants £900
13: Eight firefighters £150
PLATE 41
5: Eight men £80
7 and **8:** Officer, pioneer and six men £250
11-13: Officer, trumpeter and eight troopers £300
15-16: Eight infantry, officer and four troopers £500
PLATE 42
1: Officer and seven men £120
2: Officer and seven men £1000
3: Officer and seven men £1000
4: Officer and seven men £150
5: Officer and four troopers £800
6: Officer and four troopers £400
10 and **19:** Officer and six men £100
12-14: Twenty-six musicians £2,000
15 : and **16:** Officer and nine men £150
16 and **17** or **18:** Officer and eight men £100
PLATE 43
1 and **2:** Officer and seven men £150
3: Officer and seven men £120
4: Officer and seven men £500
5: Eight men £90
7: Eight men £150
10 and **14:** Officer and four troopers £90
12 and **18:** Five mounted, ten on foot £40
13: Individually boxed £30
PLATE 44
1: Officer and four troopers £250
2: Officer and seven men £150
3: Officer and seven men £400
6: Eight men £200
11: Eight men £80
12: Officer and seven men £90
13 and **14:** Officer and six men £120
16: Officer and four troopers £1000
17: Officer and seven men £250
18: Eight men £80
19: Officer and seven men £350
20: Officer and seven men £400
21 and **22:** Officer and seven men £300
PLATE 45
1: Officer and seven men £70
2: Officer and seven men £130

3: Officer and seven men £350
4 and **5:** Officer and seven men £150
6 and **7:** Officer and seven men £500
8: Eight men £250
9: Officer and seven men £120
10: Eight men £110
11: Eight men £130
13: Eight men £800
14 and **15:** Officer and seven men £200
18: Officer and four troopers £150
19: Officer and four troopers £300
PLATE 46
1: Eight men, assorted colours £250
5: Eight men £200
11: Officer and seven men £160
18: Officer and four troopers £100
PLATE 47
1: Eight men, assorted colours £60
4: Five men, assorted colours £80
5: Four each, running, marching and mounted £150
7: Eight men, assorted colours £90
8: Individually boxed £20
9: Fourteen assorted £140
13 and **14:** Six assorted £5
PLATE 48
1: Officer and seven men £2,000
2 and **3:** Officer and seven men £500
4 and **6:** Officer and seven men £300
7: Officer and nine assorted £400
8: Officer and nine assorted £300
9 and **11:** Officer and seven men £100
10: Officer and seven men £900
12: Officer and seven men £60
13: Individually boxed £20
14: Eight men £60
15 and **16:** Twelve musicians £500
17: Five troopers £90
18: Eight men £100
19: Officer and seven men £70
20: Sergeant and seven men £90
21: Eight men £600
PLATE 49
1: Officer and seven men £200
2: Officer and six men £150
3: Eight men £70
4: Eight men £60

5: Six men £40
8: Eight men £180
9: Eight men £130
10: Eight men £250
11: Eight men £250
12: Officer and seven men £200
13: Officer and seven men £1200
14: Officer and seven men £700
15: Officer and four troopers £800
17-19: Officer, colour and four men £40
PLATE 50
1: Six assorted £20
7, 18 and **20:** Fifteen assorted £70
7 and **9:** Ten assorted £40
11-14 and **16-18:** Forty-eight assorted £200
19 and **20:** Officer and five men at ease £30
PLATE 51
1-3: £200
4: Seven assorted £80
5: Individually boxed £15
6: Seven assorted £80
13: Individually boxed £20
14: Individually boxed £3
15 and **16:** Six assorted £5
PLATE 52
10-12 and **17:** Six knights with four each Crusaders and five mounted knights £30
14 and **15:** Nine mounted and twelve on foot £20
18: Individually boxed £5
19: Individually boxed £5
PLATE 53
8: Individually boxed £5
13: Six standing and three mounted £30
14 and **15:** Two knights, two squires, herald and marshal £200
18: Individually boxed £5
PLATE 54
1: Ten assorted £5
PLATE 55
8: Individually boxed £20
13: Two assorted colour-bearers and four men £50
15: Eight men £150

The price guide has been updated in line with the two year change in auction prices paid. Most of the changes have been upwards, *but only for good or excellent condition figures,* if anything, condition means more now than it ever has done, and prices for damaged or badly scratched figures are if anything somewhat reduced. The most highly sought after items recently have been large display boxes of Britains, where prices have more than doubled in two years, but boxes with damage are only fetching a tenth of the price of those in excellent condition.

Two new books have been published recently: My own "Collecting Toy Soldiers" Collins 1987 by James Opie, and "The Art of the Toy Soldier" New Cavendish 1987 by Henry Kurtz and Burtt Erhlich.

PLATE 1: ROYALTY AND YEOMEN

State occasions have made good subjects for toy soldiers. Top in popularity are the Yeomen of the Guard and Tower warders, shown **1–8**, **10–13** and **15**. **1**: Hill (1952). **2**: Timpo, walking to attend the State Coach (1953). **3**: Hill (30mm) to attend small-scale coach (1937). **4**: Cavendish, with axe (P 1959). **5**: Fylde, (1952) with halberd; the weapon normally carried by the Yeomen is the partisan, as **1–3**. **6**: Blenheim, set B23 (S 1977). **7**: Wend-Al (A 1951). **8**: Cherilea (1952). **9**: Renvoize souvenir Coronation Chair, dated 10 March 1902, made for the Coronation of Edward VII. **10**: Charbens, from set 513 (1950). **11**: Hill, Warder (1950). **12**: Britains set 1475 (1937), early yeoman with hand on hip. The tassle under the blade of the partisan is swung back, indicating that this man is walking, alongside the State Coach. **13**: Britains, later Yeoman, arm straight down, tassle hanging down, so from set 1257 (1938). **14**: Britains, set 2149 (1957), Gentleman-at-arms, extremely rare. **15**: Britains, 'New Metal' Yeoman set 7225 (D 1974). **16**: Blenheim, Chelsea Pensioner from set B20 (S 1977). The bottom row shows Queen Elizabeth II, the most popular being as Colonel-in-Chief of the Grenadier Guards, taking the salute at the Birthday Parade, Trooping the Colour as **17**, **19** and **20**. **17**: Wend-Al (A 1953). **18**: Unknown, Queen in Coronation robes (1953). **19**: Britains set 2065 (1952), with movable saluting arm. **20**: Unknown (1953). The hand holding the reins is pierced to take a painted wire baton, missing from this example.

17

PLATE 2: HOUSEHOLD CAVALRY

A series of the Household Cavalry mounted troopers made by Britains from 1893 to 1984. All were used as both Life Guards and Horse Guards. **1**: First version 'Germanic' Life Guard, set 1 (1893); early sets contained five, a gold sash representing the officer. **2**: Second version Horse Guard, set 2 (1897). **3**: Third version Life Guard (1902), now with movable arm. **4**: Later variation of the third version Horse Guard (1913), with the aiguillettes (cords with pointed ends) removed from the breastplate. **5**: Fourth version Horse Guard (1925) with further improved detail; separate ears for the horse and the saddle carbine removed. Note the tail is missing from this example. **6**: Fifth version Life Guard (1953). At this date, by a combination of different heads and horses, Britains provided five different figures in each set. One remained as **5**, the other two being as Horse Guards **7** and **8**. All had a new sword arm with gauntlet. **8** also shows a late variation in paint style (1965). Representation of eyes and mouth on the face is dropped in favour of a chinstrap. **9**: Herald, early standard-bearer (P 1955) rather battered and tail missing. Herald was purchased by Britains in 1959, and marketed alongside Britains' own ranges, both metal and plastic. Herald figures were always plastic and, from 1966 until the end of their production in 1975, were made in Hong Kong. **10**: Herald, later Life Guard set 7805 (1967) made in Hong Kong. The same figure had been made in Britain for some years before this. **11**: 'Eyes Right' Life Guard set 7830 (P 1968). Britains' 'Eyes Right' figures were intended to replace their best-quality metal figures. **12**: 'New Metal' Life Guard (D 1984). The latest in a ninety year series, this die-cast model with plastic parts is larger (60mm) than the standard scale.

18

PLATE 3: HOUSEHOLD CAVALRY

All Britains except **11** and **12**. **1–4** show the officers to go with **Plate 1**: 1–8. **1**: First version 'prancing horse' officer, in this instance with a special head, as issued in 1897 for set 72, Life Guards Past and Present. The same figure with the normal head as on the next figure was used for sets 1 and 2 from 1895. **2**: Second version Life Guard officer (1906) with movable arm. **3**: Third version Horse Guard officer (1910), dated 19.10.1909 (the copyright date of the master figure) underneath the base. **4**: Fourth version Life Guard officer, set 1 (1953). Set 2, the Horse Guards, retained the 'prancing horse' type of officer. **5**: Third version Horse Guard trumpeter, set 93 (1924). **6**: Early 'blue' movable arm bandsman, set 101, Band of the 1st Life Guards (1911). **7**: Later figure from the same set (1953), the model modified with no sword and reins leading to the stirrups. A similar band was made in the 'Eyes Right' range. **8**: State trumpeter, set 2085 (1954), the Musical Ride. **9**: Sovereign's Standard of the Life Guards, set 2067 (1954). **10**: Regimental trumpeter of the Life Guards, Picture Pack 1325B (1954). Picture Packs were a series of individually boxed figures. **11** and **12**: These are not Britains figures, but quite close copies of **Plate 2**: 2, done by rival firms. Britains took action against such 'piracies', preparing the way under contemporary copyright law by putting the date of creation of the master figure under the base of all models made from 1900 until 1912 when the law was changed. Piracy remained a problem, as can be seen in this book. **11**: Unknown (1903), the horse's head is raised higher than on the Britains model. **12**: Unknown (1900), a close copy of Britains, but with a saddle girth modelled, where Britains has none.

19

PLATE 4: HOUSEHOLD CAVALRY

1: Reka (1900) Life Guard, incorrectly portrayed on a brown horse. **2**: BMC (Britannia Model Company), Life Guard (1908), a very nice model, completely free of any influence by Britains. **3**: Hill, Life Guard (1950), very similar to Britains, though by now Britains seemed unworried by this. **4**: Britains 2nd Life Guard, set 43 (1903). **5**: Britains Life Guard officer in winter cloak, set 400 (1930). **6**: Hill (1952), Life Guard in cloak. Few manufacturers tried to model this subject, and the Hill figure, although fixed arm, is obviously copying the Britains. **7**: Charbens, set 502 (1952), Horse Guard at the halt. A rather peculiar pose with the trooper turned sideways and the horse sporting a bright yellow saddlecloth. **8**: Timpo, Life Guard (1953) on a rather fat horse with short legs. **9**: Malleable Mouldings (P 1947), Horse Guard standard-bearer. Representative of the earliest attempt in England to make toy soldiers of plastic, the master figure, by Holger Eriksson, was carved from wood which accounts for its somewhat chunky appearance. The detail on the standard is so intricate as to suggest that this example has been repainted. **10**: Crescent, Life Guards kettledrummer (1954). The drummer and drums are cast as one piece, and lift off the horse. Crescent have got the uniform hopelessly wrong: the horse is brown, the helmet black and the drummer is wearing a cuirass. **11**: Fylde, Life Guard at the halt (1954). Fylde were a small company started by ex-employees of Hill in Fylde in Lancashire. This figure has a movable arm. **12**: Timpo, Horse Guard mounted on a grey horse at the halt (1954). The casting for the removable trooper is the same as for **8** above.

20

PLATE 5: HOUSEHOLD CAVALRY

The popularity of the Household Cavalry prompted toy soldier makers to issue many different types. In this plate are seen dismounted State Trumpeters **1** and **6**; Britains small-size figures **2–5**; and various sentries as seen in Whitehall, **7–23**. **1**: Charbens, set 512 (1953). **2**: Gilt miniature Life Guard later used in set 13w (30mm 1901). **3**: Second-grade paint (43mm 1908). **4**: Second-grade paint (43mm 1902). **5**: Gilt (43mm 1896). **6**: Crescent (1954). **7**: Britains, mounted Horse Guard at the halt, Picture Pack 1336B (1954). **8**: Britains, Life Guard sentry, set 2029 (1949). **9**: Herald, Life Guard regimental trumpeter, set H7808 (P 1955). **10**: Britains, 'New Metal' Life Guard, set 7225 (D 1974). **11**: Unknown, copy of a Herald Life Guard (P 1957). **12**: Crescent, Life Guard, a rather thin model, very susceptible to metal fatigue (D 1946). **13**: Crescent, Life Guard, a rather better model than its predecessor (1948). **14** and **15**: Hill, the same model in different scales, **14** (42mm 1953) **15** (54mm 1950). **16**: Crescent, Life Guard in a larger than normal size (65mm 1935). **17**: Cherilea, Horse Guard at attention, set S/203 (1952). Cherilea was another northern England company, started by Wilfred Cherrington, a freelance master figure designer, and John Lee, the ex-sales manager of Hill. Cherilea is a combination of their surnames. The new company considerably outlasted Hill. **18**: Crescent, Horse Guard at attention, the same casting as **13**, looking different because of the later paint style (1948). **19**: Benbros, Life Guard, the helmet painted black (1954). **20**: Timpo, Life Guard, set 335 (1952). **21**: Charbens, Life Guard, set 509 (1950). **22**: Lone Star, early plastic Life Guard (P 1956). As usual with plastic figures the paint peels off very easily. **23**: Cherilea, Life Guard (P 1962) a large (65mm) later-style figure.

PLATE 6: FOOT GUARDS

1–8 show various marching Foot Guards made by Britains. **1**: Foot Guard, second-grade paint, set 701A (1936). **2**: First version 'valise pack' Scots Guard, set 75 (1897). **3**: Second version 'box pack' Scots Guard, set 75 (1905). **4**: Irish Guard, set 107 (1908), square base. The arm with the rifle without bayonet is rare. **5**: Third version '1910' marching figure, Grenadier Guards Colour Sergeant, set 460 (1933). This model was the standard Britains marching figure from 1910 to 1966, with many different heads and uniforms. **6**: 'Eyes Right', Scots Guard at the slope (P 1961). **7**: 'Eyes Right', Scots Guard with F. N. rifle at the shoulder, set 7228 (P 1964), note the thinner base. **8**: 'New Metal' Scots Guard, set 7225 (D 1973). He looks larger because of the thick base and large bearskin, but is still 54mm scale. Marching Foot Guards are the most numerous type of toy soldier made in Great Britain. Those shown below and opposite are just a sample of the enormous variety to be collected. **9**: Renvoize (1900), Foot Guard, bayonet missing. **10**: Unknown (1905), Foot Guard, fixed arm rifle with sling. **11**: Unknown (1920), Grenadier Guard, movable arm. **12**: Taylor and Barratt (1938), fixed arm Foot Guard. **13**: Metasol (1948), Welsh Guard. **14**: Benbros (1954), Grenadier Guard. **15**: Unknown (1935), Foot Guard. **16**: Fylde (1954), Grenadier Guard. **17**: Crescent (1949), Foot Guard. **18**: Crescent (1955), Foot Guard. **19**: Authenticast (S 1945), Irish Guard, made in Eire, mostly for export to the USA. Holger Eriksson was the sculptor – compare with **20**. **20**: Malleable Mouldings (P 1947), one of the first plastic figures made. **21**: Cherilea, Grenadier Guard (50mm P 1955) plastic figure based on a previous hollow-cast figure – see **Plate 7: 16**. **22**: Lone Star, Grenadier Guard (P 1956), very similar to Herald. **23**: Blenheim, set H10 (S 1980) Scots Guard, the head turned towards the Queen at Trooping the Colour. **24**: Matching officer for **23**, at the salute.

PLATE 7: FOOT GUARDS

1–3 show three versions of the Scots Guard piper from Britains' set 69. **1**: (1897), **2**: (1934) and **3**: (1938). **4**: Britains, Irish Guards piper from set 2123 (1957). **5**: Britains, from the same set, Irish Guards officer with drawn sword. **6**: Timpo, Grenadier Guard from set 302 (1952). **7**: Amazingly similar to **6**, this is a Sacul Grenadier Guard. Both **6** and **7** have flock-sprayed bearskins, making them fuzzy to touch. **8**: Early Timpo (1955), plastic Guards officer, obviously in the same design tradition as **6**. The paint adheres none too well to this type of plastic. **9**: Renvoize (1902), marching at the trail. **10–12**: Unknown; the distinction between Guards and Fusiliers is slight in some of these figures. **10** is 57mm scale, **11** 60mm; **10** and **12** have their movable arms missing (1900). **13**: BMC, smaller (50mm) size (1905). **14**: Unknown, Grenadier Guard made of pressed tinplate, lithographed (1930). **15**: Reka (1900), Coldstream Guard. **16**: Cherilea (50mm 1952), Foot Guard, this example has been repainted. The bottom row are all standard-bearers. **17**: Britains 'Eyes Right' Scots Guard regimental Colour from set 7226 (P 1962). **18** and **19**: Britains, regimental and King's Colours of the Grenadier Guards from set 460 (1933). **20**: Metasol (1950), Scots Guard Regimental Colour. **21**: Unknown (1930), King's Colour. **22**: Grenadier Guards King's Colour to match **14** above (1930, tinplate). **23**: Unknown (1935), King's Colour. **24**: Herald, Foot Guard from set H4207 Queen's Colour (P 1955). The only reason for calling a Colour King's rather than Queen's is the presence of a king rather than a queen on the British throne at the date quoted.

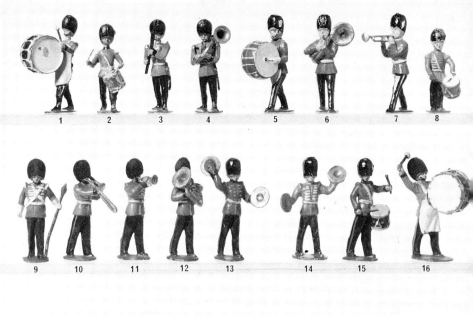

PLATE 8: FOOT GUARDS

This and the following plate show examples of Foot Guard Bandsmen, these being by far the most popular subject among manufacturers for military music. **1–4**: Britains, Coldstream Guards from set 37 (1895). These are fixed-arm figures, **3** and **4** being 'slotted-arm' bandsmen. **4** carries a bombardon, an instrument Britains did not manufacture after 1911, when all their bands were given movable arms. **5–7**: Benbros, Grenadier Guards, this set being unusual in that it too contained a bombardon (1950). **8**: Benbros, drummer boy at attention (1950). **9–13, 15** and **16**: Timpo, Grenadier Guards from set 352 (1951). The only figure on this row which is not Timpo is **14**, which is a Wend-Al Coldstream Guard. The style is very similar, and Wend-Al did buy some Timpo moulds and convert them for aluminium casting (A 1952). The Timpo band is quite attractive. **9–12** and **16** have flock-sprayed bearskins, which gives them a furry rather than a shiny appearance. The base drum of **16** is removable. **17**: Crescent (1930). **18**: Crescent (1951). **19–22**: Unknown (1910). **23** and **24**: Crescent (1930). This row is typical of the poor quality Guards bandsmen which are always turning up in job lots of toy soldiers. Determining their manufacturers is usually very tricky, since most of them were sold loose, totally unmarked, via wholesalers to small shops.

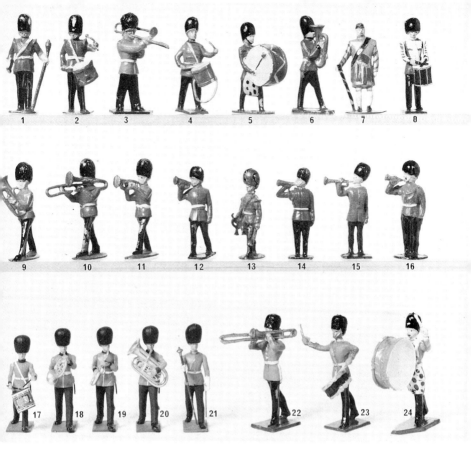

PLATE 9: FOOT GUARDS

1 and **2**: Harvey (1950), Grenadier Guards. Harvey joined Die Casting Machine Tools Ltd (D.C.M.T.), and under the Lone Star trade mark produced the Harvey series of plastic toy soldiers. **3**: Lone Star (P 1955). **4**: Fylde (1952); not many toy manufacturers attempted to reproduce drum cords. **5** and **6**: Unknown (1950), copies of Hill. **7**: Drum Major in State Dress, possibly by Halberd (1952); the top of the mace is missing. **8**: Blenheim, drummer from set H6, Pipes and Drums of the Irish Guards (1979). **9–11**: Charbens (1948), Grenadier Guards; the plume is painted on the wrong side of the bearskin. **12–16** are all buglers. **12**: Crescent (1950). **13**: Reka (1900), copy of Britains. **14**: Crescent (1930). **15**: Crescent (1930). **16**: Unknown (1927). **17–21**: Britains 'Eyes Right' bandsmen, considered by many to be the finest models of bandsmen ever made. The brass instruments are lead plated with brass, and plug into the plastic arms at the wrist. Heads and arms are movable, as is the Drum Major's wrist, enabling a wide variety of signals to be posed. These examples are Scots Guards from set 7244 (P 1962). **22–24**: In its later days, Cherilea produced rather larger-scale figures. These three are from a series of seven sold loose (65mm P 1963). **24**, the bass drummer, is comparatively rare. Most of the manufacturers of plastic toy soldiers did not go to the extra trouble of producing a bass drummer.

25

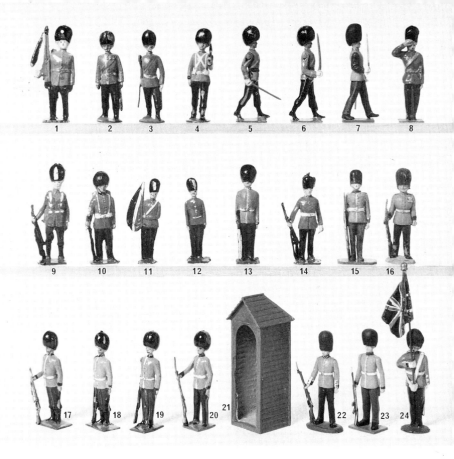

PLATE 10: FOOT GUARDS

Foot Guards have been produced in more different poses than any other sort of soldier. The following two plates show them in various drill positions. **1**: Unknown (1920), Colour-bearer at attention. The flag is not French, just an easy way of painting a furled Union Jack. **2, 3** and **5**: Britains, officers of the Scots Guards from set 75, used with the marching Guards (see **Plate 6, 1–8**). **2**: 'Bemedalled' fixed-arm officer (1897). **3**: 'Wasp-waisted' officer (1899). **5**: 'Gaitered' officer (1905). From about 1934 Britains' officers had full trousers without gaiters and no longer carried a sword. **4**: Britains, Scots Guard pioneer from set 82 (1905). **6**: Britains, Scots Guard officer from set 460 (see **Plate 6: 5** and **7, 18** and **19**) with drawn sword at attention (1934). **7**: Britains 'Eyes Right', Scots Guard officer from set 7228. This example has had its arm swopped with a blue arm from a Marine officer (P 1961). **8**: Unknown, saluting, an unusual pose. It is possible that this figure is meant to be a dismounted Scots Grey, although it was painted up as a Foot Guard (1930). **9**: Unknown Grenadier at ease (1930). **10**: Benbros, at ease (1947). **11** and **12**: Crescent, die-cast Grenadiers (48mm), very fragile – they are leaning over because impurities in the metal have caused hairline crack expansion in one side more than the other (D 1946). **13**: Authenticast (Eire), Grenadier at attention (S 1946). **14**: Cherilea, at ease (50mm 1951). **15**: Malleable Mouldings, at attention (P 1947). **16**: Cavendish, Grenadier at ease (P 1962). **17**: Britains, Scots Guard at attention from set 130 (1908). **18**: Britains, Grenadier from set 111, showing the new arm (1920). **19**: Britains, new attention figure, Scots Guard (1928). **20** and **21**: Britains, set 329 Scots Guard sentry with sentry box (1929). **22**: Zang (later Herald), at ease, this example is repainted (P 1953). **23**: Britains 'Eyes Right', at ease from set 7233 (P 1964). **24**: Timpo, Grenadier Colour-bearer from set 302 (1951).

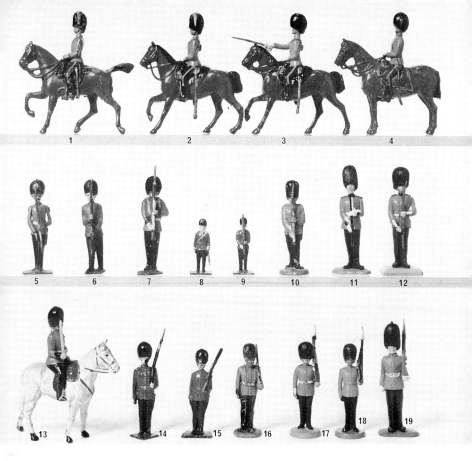

PLATE 11: FOOT GUARDS

1–4: Britains, mounted officers. **1** and **2** are Scots Grey castings painted up by Britains as Guards officers (for the equivalent Scots Greys, see **Plate 15**). **1** is probably from an early set 93 (1898), although the red Coldstream plume is painted on the wrong side of the bearskin. **2** probably comes from the double row set 56, in which a mounted officer was often included (1896). **3** is a similar Grenadier Guards officer, but with a true Foot Guards head, and the white plume painted on the wrong side. **4** is the officer on sway backed horse supplied with set 111, Grenadier Guards at attention (1901), although the plume on this example has been retouched in red. **5–12**: Foot Guards at the present. Many of these were made specifically to go with Coronation processions. **5**: Britains, Coldstream from set 205 second version (1937). **6**: Unknown (1920). **7**: Timpo, Grenadier from set 300 (1951). **8** and **9**: Hill, officer and man to go with 1937 Coronation set (30mm). **10**: Herald, from set H4205 (P 1953). **11**: Timpo, late edition, not very attractive. At this stage, Timpo were using a process whereby different coloured plastics were heat set into the mould, so that, for instance, the white gloves and cuffs are a white plastic, not simply painted on. The head and bearskin, F. N. rifle, legs and base are all separate parts (P 1978). **12**: Britains, Deetail Scots Guard from set 7255 (P 1977). Deetail figures are plastic with die-cast metal bases. **13**: Timpo, mounted officer (1953). **14–19** are all at the slope. **14**: Taylor and Barratt (1937). **15**: Unknown (1925). **16**: Herald, first version with fixed arm (P 1953). **17**: Herald, second version with movable arm (P 1955). **18**: Herald, third version with separate base and inferior painting, made in Hong Kong (P 1966). **19**: Timpo, latish edition before heat setting (P 1973).

27

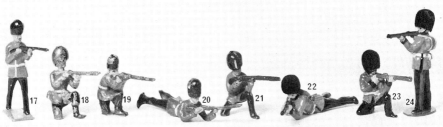

PLATE 12: FOOT GUARDS

Why there should be a fascination among manufacturers for producing Foot Guards firing weapons while wearing ceremonial dress is hard to tell, since this has not taken place since the Crimean War. Nevertheless, they are still in production at the time of writing. **1–8**: Britains. **1**: Officer with binoculars from set 130 (1906). **2–5**: Coldstream Guards from set 90. **4**: Officer with binoculars (1901). These figures are all wearing gaiters, by contrast with the next three, which have full trousers; the change took place in 1934. **6** and **7**: Coldstreams from set 90 (1934). **8**: Grenadier from set 1283 (1934). **9**: Reka, a copy of the first Britains firing figure, the 'volley firing' Foot Guard (1899). **10–12**: Unknown (1925). **13**. Reka, Coldstream (1905) a most attractive figure, one of the few produced to rival Britains. **14** and **15**: Unknown (1948). **16**: Crescent (1949). **17**: Hill (1935), this figure, and also **19**, may well have been designed as Fusiliers, from the small size of the cap. Shown here in the paint style of the 1950s, **17** was produced for many years, and even issued in plastic. **18** and **19**: Unknown (1920). **20** and **21**: Crescent, Grenadiers (1949). The white plume, which should be on the left side of the bearskin is painted on the right side of **20** and on the front of **21**. **22–24**: Timpo (1952). These figures have flock-sprayed bearskins. Timpo figures were given individual numbers for sale singly: **22** is No. 3013, **23** is No. 3012 and **24** is No. 3011. They were also on sale in set 332. Timpo, a contraction of 'Toy Importers Ltd', considered themselves in the mid 1950s to be second only to Britains in quality, with some justification as these figures show.

28

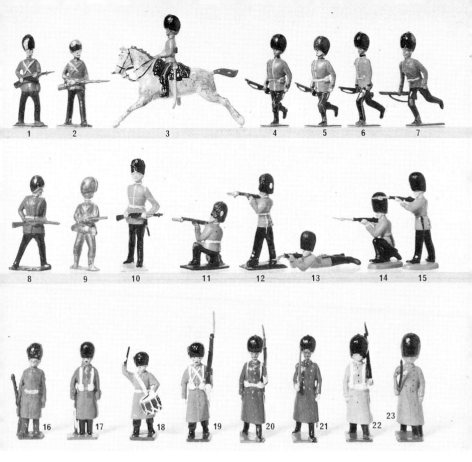

PLATE 13: FOOT GUARDS

1: Crescent, Grenadier on guard (1935). 2: Unknown (1920). 3–6: Britains. 3: Officer of the Irish Guards from set 102 (1925). 4 and 5: Scots Guards from set 130, first version with oval base (1906) and second version with square base (1908). 6: Fourth version of the same figure (1928), which because there is no space between the arm and the body is called the 'closed' elbow' version. The third version (not illustrated) has full trousers, but retains the 'open elbow' visible in 4 and 5. 7: Hill, Coldstream (1930), the red plume painted on the wrong side. 8: Crescent (1955). 9: Unknown, gilt (1910). 10: Cherilea (P 60mm 1960). 11 and 12: Lone Star, Grenadier Guards firing (P 1965). The square bases are a second version, the same models being available earlier with oval bases. They were available in set R1/5. 13–15: Herald, Foot Guards firing (P 1966). For many years the Herald range did not include firing figures, but then, when production was moved to Hong Kong, these three became available. As with many later plastic figures by Britains, the rifle barrels were apt to warp, as can be seen with 13. 16–23: Foot Guards in greatcoats, an interesting subject not made by many firms. 16: Unknown (1925), painted with an incorrect red greatcoat. 17: Unknown, probably repainted (1930). 18 and 19: Blenheim, drummer boy and private of the Coldstreams from set B57 (S 1980). 20 and 21: Britains, Grenadier Guards from set 312 (1929). 22 and 23: Hill (1949), rather dumpy figures with enormous heads.

29

PLATE 14: DRAGOON GUARDS AND DRAGOONS

The most popular subject among these cavalry has always been the 2nd Dragoons, the Royal Scots Greys, which to the uninitiated look like mounted Foot Guards. The number of examples of these on this and the next page reflect the relative numbers made by the various manufacturers. **1**: Britains (1903), gilt Dragoon Guard, probably issued as a cheap market stall line, dated 12.12.1902. **2**: Britains, set 106 (1900), 6th Dragoon Guards, the Carabiniers. **3**: Unknown, 6th Dragoon Guards (1903) a fixed arm copy of a Britains 'rocking-horse' figure. **4**: Britains, set 127 (1903), 7th Dragoon Guards officer; the troopers carried slung lances. **5**: Britains 6th Dragoon Guard, a fixed-arm figure from set 8X, the X series being cheaper boxes than the ordinary numbered sets (1908). **6**: Britains, set 6S (1959), Royal Scots Grey, another second-grade set. **7**: Unknown, Scots Grey on a copy of a Britains 'rocking-horse' (1900), this time with a movable arm. **8**: Unknown, Scots Grey (1910), an extremely attractive model, the horse copied from Britains' Royal Horse Artillery officer (see **Plate 27**: 1). **9**: Crescent, Scots Grey bandsman (1952), the white britches and brown horse being incorrect for the regiment. **10**: Hill, Scots Grey standard-bearer (1925), the standard being solid metal with a wire pole. **11**: Cherilea, set S/112 (1949), Scots Grey, an attractive horse at the halt, although owing something to **12** as an original. **12**: Hill, Scots Grey trumpeter (1925). The trumpet looks like a bugle, heightening the effect of a mounted Foot Guard.

PLATE 15: DRAGOON GUARDS AND DRAGOONS

1: Unknown, Dragoon Guard (48mm 1910), a most unusual smaller-size figure, possibly by BMC. **2**: Britains, set 6B (43mm, 1898), Scots Grey in small size. Britains smaller-size cavalry came four in a box for 6d (six old pennies, 2½p), but were still painted to the same high standard as the larger figures, and also had movable arms. **3**: Britains, a second-grade 1st Dragoon (1900). **4**: Unknown, Dragoon Guard (1930) in a completely indecipherable uniform without any resemblance to an actual regiment. **5–10**: Britains, Scots Greys. **5**: set 32, first version (1895), an early variation with a Foot Guard head. **6**: Set 32, first version (1896) with the correct Scots Grey head. **7**: Set 32, second version, short rein variation (1902) shown here in the paint style of the 1940s. **8**: Trumpeter, Picture Pack 1344B (1954), moustache added by the purchaser. The model is the same as **7** but with longer reins. **9**: Dismounted at attention, set 2119 (1959). **10**: 'Plug shoulder' Germanic Scots Grey (58mm 1894). The arm is movable, attached to a plug which runs through the body to the opposite shoulder. A very rare early figure, this example has been repainted. **11**: BMC, Scots Grey (58mm 1906), a splendid model. **12**: BMC, 1st Dragoon Guard (58mm 1906) using the same model as **11**. **13**: Unknown, 1st Dragoon Guard (1925), a copy of a Britains 'prancing horse' (tail missing) with a rather unwieldy lance.

31

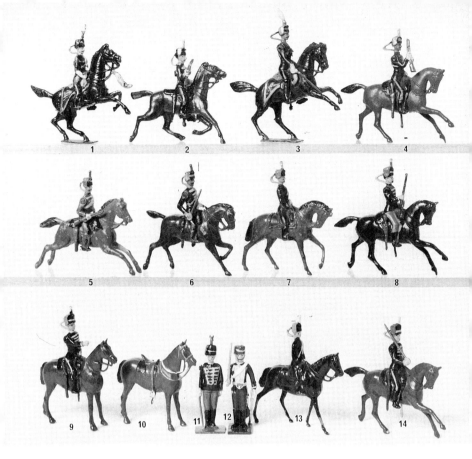

PLATE 16: HUSSARS

All except **12** are Britains. 1–4: 3rd Hussars, set 13. **1**: Officer on first version 'prancing horse' with throat plume (1894), fixed arm, tin sword. **2**: Trooper on 'donkey horse' (1894), fixed arm. **3**: Officer on third version 'prancing horse' (1909), movable arm. **4**: Trooper with short carbine on cantering horse (1903), movable arm. **5**: Set 83, Middlesex Yeomanry, first version on 'rocking-horse' (1898), an unusual set which contained 'donkey horses' (see **2** above) as well. **6**: Set 99, 13th Hussars on 'pony horse' (1899). This type of horse was only issued 1899–1903 and is quite rare. **7**: 3rd Hussar, second-grade paint, on 'head-down spindly horse' (1900), the horse's nickname comes from the much thinner legs on the fixed arm moulding. **8**: 11th Hussar, set 12, second version, cantering horse (1903). This horse was used for various sets from 1902 to 1966. **9**: 10th Hussar, set 315 (1929). **10** and **11**: 11th Hussar dismounted with horse, set 182 (1914). **10**: The attractive riderless horse which looks so good with any dismounted cavalry figure. **11**: Officer with drawn sword, the troopers in the set having empty hands. **12**: Blenheim, Gloucestershire Hussar (S1978) a short-lived model of a yeomanry regiment. **13**: 3rd Hussar, second-grade paint, on 'head-up spindly horse' (1910), shown here with 1940s-style paint. **14**: 7th Hussar, set 2075 (1953).

32

PLATE 17: HUSSARS

1: Copy of a Britains 'rocking-horse' (1898) possibly made by the German firm, Heinrich. **2**: Reka, 11th Hussar (1925). **3** and **4**: Probably Hanks copies of Britains 'pony horses', 13th Hussars, **3** with a fixed arm, and **4** with movable arm. **5**: Fylde (1954), 11th Hussar on a grey horse. The busby was not moulded with a plume. **6**: Taylor and Barratt (1937), 13th Hussar. **7**: Hill (1948), 11th Hussar with movable arm. **8**: Hill (1925), the original 11th Hussar with fixed arm, set 17/24, shown here in officer's paint style on a grey horse about 1950. In contrast to Britains, Hill and other firms were constantly changing their set numbering schemes. **9**: Crescent, Hussar (1952). As usual with Crescent, no major attempt has been made to represent a particular regiment. This series of mounted figures was based on one horse with various removable riders (see also **Plate 14**:9). **10**: Benbros, copying the Britains 'prancing horse', but painting their Hussar officer in very odd colours: brown busby, red jacket and white britches, with a green saddlecloth and yellow edging. Although this model was produced in 1952, it is copying a Britains model of 1906. **11**: Unknown, somewhat crude 60mm model of a 4th Hussar (1910). **12**: Wend-Al, 11th Hussar officer (60mm A 1952). This was one of the finest products of Wend-Al, but still keeps the chunky appearance associated with sand-cast aluminium.

PLATE 18: LANCERS

Lancers are a very popular subject among collectors, but as with Hussars, manufacturers other than Britains did not produce many. All on this page are Britains except **2–4**. **1**: 'Plug shoulder' Germanic 16th Lancer (50mm 1893). No set number was ever given to this short-lived early set. **2**: Unknown, 12th Lancer, very similar to **1** (1897). The arm is missing, showing a conventional stud shoulder rather than a hole for a plug. **3**: Heinrich, 16th Lancer, made in Germany in the British hollow-cast style (1897). **4**: Cherilea, set S/120 (1951), not representative of a particular regiment. **5**: Set 94, 21st Lancers in steel helmets (1916), the lance pennon is represented as furled by clipping off the pennon casting. **6**: Set 94, the trumpeter to go with **5** (1914). **7**: Set 24, 9th Lancer officer (1894). This is one of Britains best-loved figures, and was in production from 1894 to 1966, used as the officer for all sets of lancers at the halt. The officer should be holding a tin sword, often missing, as in this example. **8**: 9th Lancer, sold as an individual second-grade painted figure, 9c (1928). **9**: Set 23, 5th Irish Lancer (1903), this being the normal trooper for all lancers at the halt. **10**: Set 33, 16th Lancers (1903), this one being unusual as he has a slung lance. **11** and **12**: Set 23, 9th Lancers (1894), first version on 'cross-legged' horses, the difference between the two being the shape of the head which shows that **12** is a good restoration with a replaced head. These two also demonstrate the difference between GOOD paint condition (**11**), and FAIR paint condition (**12**).

34

PLATE 19: LANCERS

1 and **2**: Britains, 12th Lancers, set 128 (1903). This set normally used slung lances, but sometimes they were at the carry, as **2**, or contained both. **3**: Britains, 12th Lancer, set 1A, second-grade (1926), on 'head-down spindly horse'. **4**: Britains, 16th Lancer (1950). This figure was never issued in a set, but was made to order. Figures made only to special order are known as 'Britains Specials', and could be new combinations of head and body moulds, or simply 'Special Paint'. **5**: Crescent (1950). As so often with Crescent, this uniform follows no known regiment, but there is a correctly shaped Lancer cap. **6**: F. G. Taylor, 17th Lancer (1950), a clear copy of a Britains figure (see **3** above). **7**: Fylde, 12th Lancer (1953), the design probably most under the influence of Hill. **8**: Hill, 12th Lancer, set 17/23 (1922). **9**: Wend-Al, 12th Lancer officer (60mm A 1952). **10**: BMC, 12th Lancer (1908) a very spirited and original figure. **11**: Britains, 21st Lancer with sword (1950), an unusual figure not from any known set. The white plume has almost faded into the background of the picture. **12** and **13**: Benbros, Lancers on foot at attention (1951). Very few toy manufacturers produced dismounted Lancers, although many have been done since for collectors. The uniforms here are: **12**, blue jacket, red trousers, white plastron, and **13**, red jacket, blue trousers and plastron. The latter presumably represents the 16th Lancers, although the blue is much too light. The former represents no known regiment.

35

PLATE 20: HIGHLANDERS

Highlanders are an ever-popular subject. The top row shows charging Highlanders (see also **Plate 33**). The original Britains first version are on the right. **1**: Lord Roberts Workshop, Black Watch in glengarry, bayonet missing (1910). **2–4**: Britains, the usual charging figure (1903). Even in black and white the regiments are easily distinguished by the sporran: **2**, set 15, Argylls, two white tails on a grey sporran, **3** and **4**, set 11, Black Watch, two black tails or five tassels on a white sporran. **3** is an officer, having gold facings rather than the normal blue as **4**. **5** and **6**: Copies of Britains plug-handed figure **7**. **5**: Renvoize, Black Watch (1900). **6**: Unknown, possibly Reka Gordon (1900). **7**: Britains, set 77, Gordon (1897). **8**: Britains, officer for the same set. **5–8** all have hands holding weapons which plug into the arms at the wrist, hence 'plug-handed', a technique introduced by Britains for set 11 in 1893. **9–16** are Britains Highlanders on parade. **9** and **10**: Officers of the Gordons, set 437 (1933). **11**: Seaforth, first version marching figure with 'box pack' set 112 (1901). **12**: Gordon, set 77 (1912). **13**: The same figure with a new arm casting with plaid; Colour Sergeant, Colour Party of the Black Watch, set 2111 (1955). **14**: Herald, set H7102, Gordon (P 1955). **15**: 'New Metal' Gordon, set 7245 (D 1983). **16**: Herald, Gordon H100 (P 1955). **17**: BMC, Gordon (50mm 1908). **18**: BMC (60mm 1908), the tartan, white over blue, does not suggest any specific regiment. **19**: Wellington Toy Company, Gordon Officer (1920). **20**: Unknown, Black Watch (1925). **21**: Renvoize, Black Watch (1905). **22**: Unknown, Black Watch (1935).

PLATE 21: SCOTTISH TROOPS

This page includes models of the Lowland Regiments, but the top of the page continues the theme of marching Highlanders. **1**: Hill, early Black Watch with fixed bayonet (1920). **2**: Hill, later Black Watch set 17/3 (1930). Hill insisted on giving their otherwise correctly coloured Black Watch a yellow striped tartan. **3** and **6**: Benbros, the more detailed painting on **6** giving it a completely different appearance. **4**: Crescent, Gordon (1948). **5**: Charbens, Gordon (1947). **7**: Timpo, Gordon, an early plastic 'bemedalled' figure (P 1955). **8**: Cherilea, Argyll, early plastic figure (P 1956). **9** and **10**: Unknown, Camerons, lithographed tinplate (1930, see also **Plate 7**: 14 and 22). **11**: Fylde, Black Watch officer (1953). **12**: MSR, Black Watch. **13**: Wend-Al, Black Watch (60mm A 1950). **14**: Unknown, similar to BMC, Black Watch in glengarry (1910). **15**: Britains, set 212, piper of the Royal Scots (a Lowland regiment), issued in sets from 1948. **16**: Britains, Royal Scot, set 212 (1924). **17**: Britains, Highland Light Infantry, set 213 (1924); in spite of its name, this is a Lowland regiment. **18**: Britains, Cameronian Rifles Officer, set 1913 (1940); this also is a Lowland regiment. **19**: Wellington Toy Company, Cameronian Rifleman (1920). **20**: Unknown, Highlander in Kilmarnock bonnet (1924). **21**: BMC, Royal Scot (60mm 1908). **22** and **23**: Hill, Royal Scots and officer (1951).

PLATE 22: HIGHLANDERS

The top two rows show Highlanders in action, nearly all wearing white foreign service helmets.
1–7: Britains, Highlanders firing and officers with binoculars. **1–6** are Gordons. **1**: Set 157,
oval based (1908). **2**: Second version of the same figure, the kilt being more flared at the back
(1934). **3**: Picture Pack 292B (1954). **4**: Set 118, officer, early variation with a smooth helmet
rather than showing the bump of the puggaree wound round it (1901). **5**: Set 157, kneeling
(1906), the second version was almost identical. **6**: Set 118, lying (1901). **7**: Set 89, Cameron
lying (1934) with feet apart rather than together as in the first version (see **6**). From this view the
difference shows in the angle of the toes and the more upright head on **7**. **8**: Hill, Black Watch
on guard (1948), a figure which blends well with Britains. **9**: Unknown, possibly Wellington Toy
Company, with blue doublet and red kilt (1920). **10**: Hill, set 17/12, larger size on guard
(60mm 1904). **11**: Hill, set 17/11 lying (60mm 1904). **12** and **13**: Blenheim, Cameron officer
and man, set B33 (S 1977). **14**: Unknown, Gordon (60mm 1920). **15**: Unknown, Gordon
machine-gunner, reminiscent of Britains set 194 (1920). **16**: Unknown, Gordon in full dress
(1950). While Foot Guards firing their weapons in full dress were often produced, most
manufacturers followed Britains in giving their fighting Highlanders the foreign service helmet.
17 and **18**: Hill, 'Monarch Series' Jacobite rebels from the '45 (P 1956). **19**: Unknown (48mm
1930). **20**: Unknown (1925). **21**: Unknown (1925). **22**: Cherilea, Gordon, set S/132 (1950).
23: Malleable Mouldings, Gordon (P 1947). **24**: Herald, Gordon in glengarry (P 1954).

PLATE 23: HIGHLANDERS

Examples of Highland musicians. Most manufacturers made pipers, but rather fewer provided matching drummers. Very few depicted Highlanders with musical instruments other than pipes. **1**: BMC (60mm 1908). **2**: Reka, Gordon (1905). **3** and **4**: Britains, set 77, Gordons. **3**: First version (1897). **4**: Second version (1912). **5**: Cherilea, Argyll set S/131 (48mm 1950). **6**: Fry, Highland dancer (48mm 1920). **7**: Plastic remould of a Crescent piper at the halt (P 1982). **8**: Benbros, Seaforth bugler (1952). **9** and **10**: Sacul, Gordons (60mm 1950). **11**: Unknown, Gordon Drum Major (60mm P 1960). **12**: Hill, Gordon (58mm 1949). **13–16**: Hill, Monarch Series (58mm 1955), a late attempt to produce some better-quality figures. It is not certain if Monarch was originally an independent firm. **17**: Soldiers' Soldiers, Black Watch piper in Foreign Service Dress, an example of a 'New Toy Soldier' made for collectors (S 1982). **18**: Timpo, Gordon (1951). **19**: Herald, set H7104 (P 1954). **20**: Unknown, Cameron tinplate piper, to match **Plate 21**: 9 and 10 (1930). **21** and **22**: Cherilea, Argyll musicians, to match **Plate 21**: 8 (48mm P 1956). **23** and **24**: Lone Star, Harvey Series musicians of the Gordon Highlanders. **23**: Drummer in metal (1955), designed and sold by Harvey before he joined Lone Star. **24**: Trombonist in plastic, produced as a Lone Star product (1958). Curiously this is the only Highland military bandsman other than pipers and drummers that I can recall ever being produced by a British manufacturer, and Harvey did no other accompanying instrumentalists.

PLATE 24: ZULU WAR

1–3: Britains, set 147, Zulus, showing the three different arms used. **1**: Raised arm with spear; **2**: arm with knobkerrie, and **3**: arm carrying spear (1906). **4**: Britains Zulu was the last of their models to be issued with an oval base, although only the difference in the width of the base can be seen here, **1–3** having rectangular bases. **5**: Britains, set 22A, second-grade Zulu with fixed arm. He is carrying a shield on the side away from the camera (1913). **6**: Hanks Brothers (1910). **7**: Unknown, British Infantry on guard in red jacket and brown foreign service helmet with puggaree (1905), a most attractive figure. **8**: Blenheim, set B25, Boer firing (S 1977). Blenheim Military Models, a leading 'New Toy Soldier' company, made a particular feature of the Zulu Wars. **9**: Blenheim, set B15 Zulu (S 1977). **10**: Hill, item 106A Zulu (1910). **11**: Lone Star, African Witch Doctor (P 1960). **12–15**: Blenheim, 24th Regiment of Foot in action (S 1977). **16**: Britains, set 81, 17th Lancer in foreign service dress as at the battle of Ulundi in 1879 (1902). **17**: Britains, set 148, Royal Lancaster Regiment in foreign service helmet with ramrod (1907). **18–25**: Blenheim, 24th Regiment of Foot (S 1980). **18**: Man putting wood on camp fire. **19**: Man seated on log, drinking tea. **20** and **21**: Medical officer examining wounded man. **22–24**: Stretcher-bearers with wounded on stretcher. **25**: Man standing with cup of tea.

PLATE 25: SUDAN CAMPAIGNS

1: Britains, Egyptian Camel Corps, set 48 (1922), second version without wire tail. **2**: Britains, from set 131, British Camel Corps (1906), first version with wire tail. The camel is the same as 1, and in this example the rider's rifle has been broken off. This figure only appeared as a nine-piece row within the massive 275-piece display set, the largest ever made by Britains. The Camel Corps was drawn from various British regiments serving in Egypt and was a popular subject for toymakers. **3** and **4**: Britains, 21st Lancers 'Heroes of Omdurman', set 94 (1901), second version on 'one-eared' horses. The lance head of **4**'s lance is missing. **5–7**: British Camel Corps by various unknown makers (1908). These were usually smaller than 54mm. **8**: RSM, British artillery officer in foreign service dress (S 1981). **9**: Britains, Egyptian cavalry, set 115 (1901), first version on 'pony horse'. **10**: Britains, Egyptian cavalry, set 115 (1903), second version on cantering horse dated 12 February 1903. **11**: Britains, Soudanese Infantry, set 116 (1901), first version with oval base. **12**: Britains, Egyptian Infantry, set 117 (1901), first version with round base. This example is coloured dark-blue, a rare early paint variation. Later models were coloured French grey. **13**: Unknown, Egyptian infantry in winter dress (1925). **14**: Reka, Egyptian infantry in summer dress (1900).

PLATE 26: BOER WAR

1: Britains, 6th Dragoons, set 108 (1900). The same model provided with a slouch hat was used for set 105, the Imperial Yeomanry. **2**: Unknown, Imperial Yeomanry cavalry (1901). **3**: Britains, Boer Cavalry, set 6 (1897). The same model in different colours was used for the South African Mounted Infantry, set 38. **4**: Blenheim, Imperial Yeomanry officer, set C1 (S 1974). **5–10**: Britains. **5**: City Imperial Volunteer, set 104 (1900). **6**: Gloucestershire Regiment, set 119 (1901). **7**: Devonshire Regiment, set 110 (1901), first version at the slope with smooth, foreign service helmet. **8**: Devonshire Regiment, set 110 (1937), fourth version, with Wolseley helmet and webbing equipment, as they would have appeared during the Mesopotamia campaign, in the First World War, an example of Britains' updating a set. **9**: special set manufactured for CFE, Army Service Supply Column. The figure is the same as **7** with a different head and arm. **10**: York and Lancaster Regiment, set 96 (1898) depicting the Sudan campaign, but just as valid for the Boer War. **11**: Blenheim, Coldstream Guard, set B26 (S 1978). **12**: Renvoize, Imperial Volunteer (1906). **13–16**: Britains, set 114, Cameron Highlanders in foreign service dress, in reverse order of version. **16**: First version (1901) with smooth helmet. **15**: Second version with puggaree (1903). **14**: Third version with new body (1922). **13**: Fourth version with new head (1937). **17–20**: Britains, set 26, Boer Infantry. The first version is **19** (1899), usually found at the slope. **17** and **18**: Two new figures used for the set from 1906. **20**: Officer that went with sets of **17**.

42

PLATE 27: ROYAL ARTILLERY (RA)

1–8: Britains. **1**: Royal Horse Artillery (RHA) officer, set 39 (1895), the officer's tall plume is missing. **2**: Set 39, mounted RHA gunner, four of which replaced the gunners seated on the limber and gun (1906). **3**: Royal Field Artillery (RFA) officer, set 144 (1906). **4**: RFA service dress, officer, set 144a (1916). **5**: RHA at the halt, team horse with driver, set 316 (1924). **6**: RA gun with gunners, officer, set 1289 (1934). **7**: RA in steel helmets, officer, set 1730 (1948). **8**: Small RA gun, No. 1263 (1933). Britains made many cannon to support their troops. This is the smallest and cheapest of the Royal Artillery guns. **9**: Bulldog 'New Toy Soldier' RA sergeant from a mountain gun crew (S 1976). **10**: Marktime, RHA officer (S 1975). **11–13**: Crescent, kneeling gun crew (1938). **14**: Skybird, anti-aircraft artillery officer (25mm S 1937). **15**: Britains, spotting chair with spotter, set 1731 (1939). **16**: Hill, spotting chair with spotter (1939). **17** and **18**: Crescent, anti-aircraft heightfinder and operator (1939). **19** and **20**: Crescent, sound locator and operator (1939). **21**: Crescent, anti-aircraft artillery officer (1939). Just before the second World War, considerable interest was taken in anti-aircraft defences. Both Crescent and Britains produced a full range of equipment, the Crescent being the rarer to survive.

43

PLATE 28: INFANTRY OF THE LINE

These are toy soldiers in the full dress uniform with spiked helmet of the ordinary British Army infantry of the period 1890 to 1914. Many were manufactured during that period and later, and they all look rather alike. After the Second World War, their popularity waned, and few were made other than by Britains. **1**: Britains, set 25 (1895), soldier with hollow gun and spring which propels a piece of wire through the barrel. **2** and **3**: Bemedalled officers. **2**: Hanks, copy of **3** (1898). **3**: Britains, Royal West Surrey Regiment, set 29 (1895). **4**: Set 29, as **3** (1895) is the earliest example of Britains infantry at the slope, but with the rifle on the wrong shoulder. **5**: Hanks, a similar figure with movable arm (1900). **6**: Britains, Worcestershire Regiment, second grade (1895). **7**: Britains, Worcestershire Regiment, set 18 (1910), second version. **8**: Britains East Yorkshire Regiment, set 113 (1925), third version. **9** and **10**: Britains, set 29 as **3**. **9**: Second version 'valise pack' (1897), bayonet missing. **10**: Third version 'box pack' (1905). **11**: Britains, W series (45mm 1930). **12**: BMC (60mm 1908). **13** and **14**: Abel (1900); **13** has a base shaped to slot into a mechanical parade toy. **15**: Unknown (60mm 1925). **16**: Unknown (48mm 1925). **17–20** and **22**: Britains. **17**: Warwickshire Regiment, set 206 (1922). **18** and **19**: Royal West Surrey Regiment, set 121 (1908). **20**: as **6** but standing. **21**: Unknown, inferior copy of **20** (1900). **22**: As **3**, second version (1910). **23**: Taylor and Barratt (1937). **24**: Britains 'Eyes Right' Middlesex Regiment, set H 4163 (P 1960).

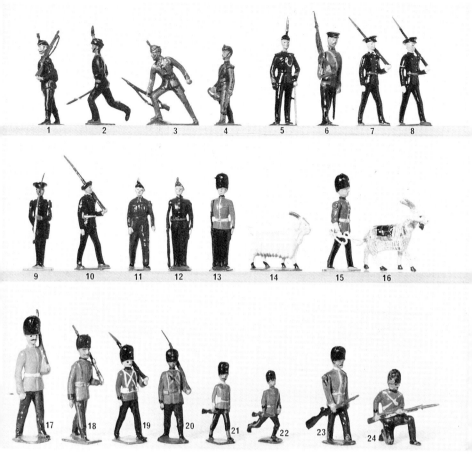

PLATE 29: BRITISH ARMY REGIMENTS, FULL DRESS

All Britains except **3, 6, 15, 16, 23** and **24**. **1**: Rifle Brigade, first version, set 9 (1897). **2**: King's Royal Rifle Corps (KRRC) officer, set 98 (1922), third version 'open elbow'. **3**: BMC, KRRC (1905). **4**: Rifle Brigade boy bugler (1900), plume and mouthpiece missing. **5**: set 1908, Infantry officers, officer of the KRRC (1940) based on the medical figure (see **Plate 30**: 17 and 18). **6**: Unknown (58mm 1908). **7**: Made especially for a 1953 mechanical Coronation procession. **8**: Gloucestershire Regiment, set 2089 (1954). The blue armband commemorates a UN unit citation in the Korean War. **9**: Territorials, green uniform, set 1541 (1937). **10**: Parachute Regiment, set 2092 (1954). **11** and **12**: Royal Irish Fusiliers. **11**: Special in service dress (1953). **12**: Set 2090 (1954). **13** and **14**: Royal Welch Fusilier with goat mascot, set 2124 (1957). **15** and **16**: Hill, Royal Welch Fusilier handler with mascot (1951). The next six figures show different sizes made by Britains. **17**: No. 5h large-size Fusilier, second-grade paint (70mm 1910). **18**: Un-numbered very early 'plug-handed' Royal Fusilier (60mm 1893). **19**: Royal Welch Fusilier, standard size, set 74 (54mm 1949) fifth version. **20**: Royal Fusilier with 'valise pack', set 7 (52mm 1897). **21**: Lancashire Fusilier, second version, set 17b (45mm 1912). **22**: Dublin Fusilier, first version, set 19b (43mm 1898). **23**: Unknown, Fusilier (1910). **24**: BMC, Fusilier (60mm 1908).

PLATE 30: STAFF AND SERVICE CORPS

Relatively few staff and service corps toys have been made, since boys have generally preferred 'real' soldiers. Medical Corps figures, however, have always been one of Britains' most popular lines. **1–6**: Britains, Staff Officers. **1, 5** and **6**: Set 201, Officers of the General Staff. **1**: General Officer (1922). **2** and **3**: General Staff in khaki, red arm and cap bands denote Staff, set 1907 (1940). **4**: Infantry officers, set 1908, (1940) see also **Plate 29**: 5. **5**: General Officer with binoculars (1922) shown here in the paint style of the 1950s. **6**: Aide-de-camp (1922). **7** and **8**: Hill, General Officers (1925). **9**: Hill, General (30mm 1937) to go with Hill Coronation procession sets. **10**: Steadfast, General (S 1977). **11**: Britains, railway figures, military policeman, set 1R (1954). This figure is made with the Militia body (compare **Plate 34**: 3) and a peak cap head, appropriately painted. **12–19**: Britains, Army Medical Service, set 137 (1905). **12** and **15**: Stretcher-bearers, oval based, carrying **13**: Man with leg wound on **14**: stretcher. **16**: Nurse, first version. **17**: Senior medical officer. **18**: Doctor. **19**: Man with head wound. **20**: Britains, another man with head wound, painted khaki to go with set 1723, Royal Army Medical Corps in steel helmets (1939). **21**: Britains, woman driver from Motor Ambulance with medical personnel, set 1897 (1940).

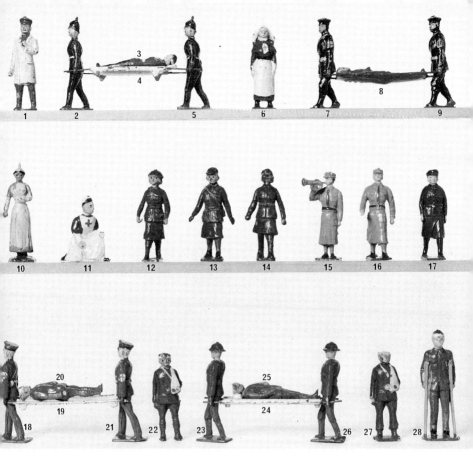

PLATE 31: MEDICAL, WOUNDED, NURSES AND AUXILIARIES

1: Hill, No. 682, doctor (1920). 2–6: Hill, set RX2, Red Cross set, full dress RAMC stretcher-party with nurse (1920). 7–9: Kew, stretcher-party (1925). Here the stretcher and casualty are moulded as one piece. This item was produced in blue, khaki or white according to context, full dress, service dress or civilian. 10: Fry, nurse (1914). 11: Hill, kneeling nurse (1905). 12: Crescent, Auxiliary Territorial Service (ATS), presumably the hand is shaped to carry a bucket (1940). 13: Hill, ATS (1940). 14: Unknown, ATS (1940), whose head has been turned by someone! This is as originally moulded and not a conversion. 15 and 16: Taylor and Barratt, ATS (1940). 17: Britains, nurse in khaki, wearing a similar uniform to an AT, set 1897 (1940). Britains never produced a set of ATS, their Army ladies being confined to nurses and the driver from the same set (see **Plate 30**: 21). 18–21: Crescent, stretcher-party (1928). 22: Crescent, the same casualty as shown lying on the stretcher is shown here standing up, which he is able to do on his two moulded feet in a wobbly fashion. 23–26: Taylor and Barratt, stretcher-party (1935). Note the puttees, which changed to gaiters on the introduction of battledress. 27: Unknown, another casualty similar to 22 (1939). He is provided with a base, so stands well, but cannot lie on a stretcher. 28: Charbens, man on crutches (60mm 1936), an unusually large-scale figure from this firm.

47

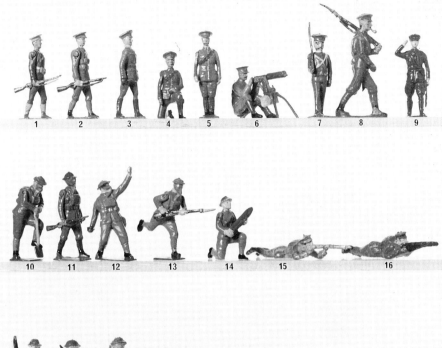

PLATE 32: FIRST WORLD WAR

The Great War produced a lasting anti-war feeling in Britain, but during the next twenty years many models of combatants were produced as toys — some in the initial outburst of patriotic feeling of 1914–15. **1–6**: Britains. **1**: Territorials, set 160 (1909), in Slade Wallace equipment. **2**: The same set, with webbing equipment (1916), retitled British Expeditionary Force. **3**: Officer for **2**. **4** and **5**: RA gunners, service dress, set 313 (1929). **6**: Machine-Gun Section, sitting, set 198 (1920). This is the first version with a Maxim gun. The later version was distinctively equipped with a Vickers gun with a thinner barrel. **7**: Hanks, Territorial (1912). **8**: BMC, an attractive fixed-arm figure marching along with a pipe in his mouth (62mm 1914). **9**: Taylor and Barratt, officer saluting (1930). **10–13**: Britains, infantry in gas masks. **10**: The energetic man digging a trench only appeared in larger sets such as No. 1614 (1937). **11**: This set of marching figures appeared years before the others, set 258 (1928). **12**: Grenade thrower, set 1612 (1937). **13**: Charging, set 1613 (1937). **14**: Britains, artilleryman with shell, second-grade paint (1939). **15**: Hill, attractive lying figure, No. 933 (1914). **16**: Unknown (1930). **17**: Hill, No. 611 (1920). Although the flag looks like a French tricoleur, it is an attempt to show a furled Union Jack. **18**: Crescent (1930). **19**: Unknown (1930). **20**: Hill, No. 614A (1920). **21**: Crescent, man cutting barbed wire (1930). **22**: Crescent, barbed wire entanglement (1930). **23**: BMC, another attractive lying figure (60mm 1914).

48

PLATE 33: FIRST WORLD WAR

1: BMC (1914). **2**: Fry, an attractive 'Tommy' (1914). Fry in particular seemed to specialize in First World War figures, producing many at the time. **3**: Hill, No. 9A, a stubby little figure with an enormous rifle (48mm 1915). **4**: BMC, smaller-scale figure of the sort that appeared with their cardboard trench set (50mm 1915). **5**: BMC, a new head on the Fusilier figure (see **Plate 29**: 24) does duty at the front (60mm 1914). **6**: Unknown (1926). **7**: Crescent (1926). **8–12**: Highlanders in the First World War. **8**. Unknown (1925). **9**: Fry (1916). **10**: Britains (1922). **11**: Fry, London Scottish (1916). **12**: Fry, London Scottish (1917). **12** is something of an improvement on **11**, although in this example the bayonet is missing. **13**: Britains, French infantry in action, set 215 (1924). **14**: Britains, German infantry in steel helmets, set 432 (1931), this figure is all in field grey with black boots. **15**: Unknown, Prussian surrendering (45mm 1918), this figure may have been made in France. **16**: BMC, small size (45mm 1915). **17**: BMC (50mm 1915). **18**: Britains, cavalry in steel helmet, second-grade paint, here in the style of the 1950s (1925). **19**: Britains, motor cycle dispatch rider, set 200 (1922), here in the paint style of the 1930s. Earlier it was the practice to leave the metal parts of the cycle unpainted.

PLATE 34: SECOND WORLD WAR

The Second World War had less impact on Britain in terms of casualties than the First, and there were more achievements to be proud of, hence a marked increase in toy soldiers. **1–5**: Britains. **1**: Infantry in battledress, set 1858 (1939), showing the new British Army uniform introduced in that year. **2**: Air Raid Precautions (ARP) Warden, set 1914 (1940). **3**: Militia, set 1854 (1939). **4**: Set 1898 (1940) in action in battledress. **5**: No. 93N, second-grade tommy-gunner (1940). **4** and **5** were fixed-arm figures made with the second grade in mind. **6**: Hill, infantry in field cap (1939). He has a steel helmet attached to his belt behind his back. **7**: Hill, man in anti-gas suit (1939). The bayonet has a piece of litmus paper on it to indicate the presence of gas. **8**: Britains, ARP decontamination man with gas detector stick, set 1759 (1939). Britains used the wire golf club from their golfer. **9**: Taylor and Barratt, decontamination man in anti-gas suit (1939). **10–12**: Crude wartime toy soldiers. **10** and **12**: Unknown (1940). **11**: Crescent (D 1945). **13**: Taylor and Barratt, soldier with tommy-gun (1940). **14** and **15**: Crescent, men advancing. **14**: (1947). **15**: (1952) with the steel helmet painted bright green. **16**: Harvey, paratrooper (1954). **17**: Charbens, paratrooper (1954). **18–20**: Composition figures, some of the few made in Britain. **18**: TAG, educational toy (70mm 1946). **19**: Unknown (1946), the gun, made of a pin, is missing. **20**: Unknown (1946). **21**: Wend-Al (A 1950). **22**: Unknown, the box advertising 'Invincible Shock proof Toy Soldiers' (60mm S 1946). **23** and **24**: Britains, set 1859 (1939), the wartime sentry replacing the familiar Foot Guard.

PLATE 35: SECOND WORLD WAR

1–4: Timpo. **1**: British infantry officer, set B30 (1951). **2** and **3**: More figures from the same series, converted to plastic moulding (P 1954). **4**: Montgomery character figure from the Eighth Army series (P 1956). **5**: Cherilea, Montgomery character figure (60mm P 1960). **6**: Dinky Toy, Royal Tanks Corps officer, 150a (25mm D 1938). **7**: Lone Star, Harvey series R3/9 'Desert troops' Australian infantry, Eighth Army (P 1958). **8**: Britains, Scots Guard in service dress, steel helmet, set 1834 (1939). **9**: Britains, German infantry, second version, set 432 (1949), now in the Wehrmacht full dress with green helmet and jacket. **10** and **11**: Speedwell, German infantry in action (48mm P 1955) made out of a mixed colour plastic not fully stirred, thus resembling a camouflage pattern. **12** and **13**: Cherilea, German officers (60mm P 1960): **12**: European theatre; **13**: North African theatre. **14**: Cherilea, Afrika Corps infantry surrendering, hands on head (60mm P 1960). **15**: Lone Star, Afrika Korps waving white flag, set R3/10 (P 1958). A proportion of British-made German Army figures usually depicted men giving up the unequal struggle! **16** and **17**: Timpo, German infantry with removable weapons (P 1976). **18** and **21**: Timpo, Eighth Army infantry (P 1956). **19** and **20**: Charbens, Eighth Army infantry, very similar to the Timpo series (P 1959). **22**: Charbens, Paratrooper (P 1959). **23** and **24**: Lone Star, Paratroops in red berets, set R1/1 (P 1957). This series was also issued as Commandos with green berets.

PLATE 36: MODERN INFANTRY

Since the Second World War, forty years of Cold War have produced little change in the basic infantry role, and toy soldier manufacturers have continued to produce infantry in battledress, many of which are indistinguishable from Second World War types. **1**: Britains, set 56S (1953); compare **Plate 34**: 4 and **5** wearing the Mark I steel helmet, with this attempt to represent the Mark III. **2**: Zang, infantry in beret (P 1953). **3**: Herald, the more familiar figure, based on **2** with a movable arm (P 1954). **4**: Britains, Swoppet infantry, set 7330 (P 1962). **5**: Timpo, US machine-gunner (P 1956). **6**: Cherilea, paratrooper with mine detector (P 1960). **7**: Crescent, infantryman with flamethrower (P 1955). **8**: Crescent, paratroop light mortar (P 1957). **9–20**: All depict US infantry. **9**: Charbens, charging, No. 201 (1950). **10**: Charbens, with mortar, No. 216 (P 1958). **11**: Cherilea, set A/100 (1951). **12**: Cherilea, Bazooka (1952), actually fires, though not, as claimed, the first hollow-cast toy soldier to do so (see **Plate 28**: 1). **13**: Charbens, a similar machine-gun (1952). **14**: Crescent (1950). **15–17**: Crescent, mortar with crew (1950), a nice model with both crew stripped to the waist and painted bronze, presumably to represent sun-tan. **18–20**: Charbens (1950). **21**: Lone Star, paratrooper crawling (P 1955). **22–24**: Lone Star, paratroop stretcher-party (P 1956). **25**: Lone Star, paratrooper with Bren gun (1955). **26**: Crescent, anti-tank gun with two crew, all moulded in one piece (1950).

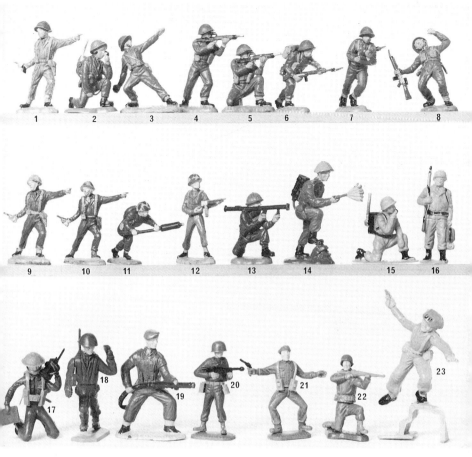

PLATE 37: MODERN INFANTRY

These are all plastic figures. **1–8**: Herald, British infantry in action, set H 7304 (P 1953). These superb figures set the standard for plastic toy soldiers, and through four versions and various paint variations were on offer from 1953 to 1975. The complete set of eight original poses is shown here, with their beautifully sculpted Mark III helmets. **2**: Fourth-version figure made in Hong Kong in a shinier plastic with removable base. This series was probably the most widely copied ever. Early models (1953) can be found with the Zang trademark (⊠) underneath the base, and all early figures have smooth helmets. Later versions have a helmet with moulded camouflage net. **9** and **10**: copies of **1**. **9**: Speedwell (P 1958). **10–12**: Hill (P 1956), Speedwell painted yellow patches on the helmet and Hill painted brown patches. Not all Hill figures were copies, **11** and **12** being original designs. **13**: Herald, later addition to the infantry, only made in Hong Kong (P 1966). **14**: Crescent (58mm P 1960). **15** and **16**: Timpo, West German infantry, a colour variation of the US Infantry (P 1959). From 1960, many firms copied Britains 'Swoppet' idea of models with interchangeable parts, of which **17–22** are examples. **17**: Cherilea (65mm P 1965). **18**: Lone Star (60mm P 1965). **19**: Lone Star paratrooper with plug-in head (62mm P 1965). **20**: Timpo, US infantry (P 1962). **21**: Timpo, paratroop officer (P 1965). **22**: Timpo, US infantry (P 1972). **23**: Cherilea, UN infantry officer (65mm P 1965) rather grotesque. Later models of infantry seemed to follow the principle that the wilder the action the better the model, but sales confirmed the popularity of the neater, more realistic figures.

53

PLATE 38: ROYAL NAVY

1–4: Britains. **1**: The running petty officer who leads sets 78, 79 and 80. **2**: Bluejacket, set 78 (1897). **3**: Whitejacket, set 80 (1897). **4**: Landing-party with gun, set 79 (1897), the string to pull the gun passes through one of the loops formed by the hands. **5**: Renvoize (1900) copy of a Britains Bluejacket. **6**: Unknown, member of landing-party to pull a gun (1902). **7** and **8**: Britains, officers and petty officers, set 207 (1923). **7**: Midshipman. **8**: Admiral. **9**: Unknown, sailor in straw hat (1905). **10**: BMC, Bluejacket (60mm 1906). **11**: Unknown (60mm 1922). **12**: Crescent (1930). **13**: Fry, Whitejacket (1916). **14**: Crescent (1930). **15** and **16**: Charbens, historical sailors to fight pirates (P 1960). **16**: Character figure of Nelson. **17**: Taylor and Barratt, No. 3505, naval guard (1937). **18**: Unknown (1935). **19**: Unknown (1935). **20**: Crescent (1935). **21**: Unknown (1935). **22** and **23**: Hill (1904). **22**: No. 47, this sailor on guard, was one of the best figures produced by Hill, and compares well with firms which consistently produced high-quality products. **23**: No. 21, the kneeling sailor, was not quite to the same standard. Best-quality painting of this figure was called 21A, and the three-colour finish shown here was 21C, costing a halfpenny less. **24**: Lone Star, set R3/12, sailor, this being an imaginative model at the wheel of a ship (P 1959).

PLATE 39: ROYAL NAVY

1–8: Britains. **1–4**: Set 97, Royal Marine Light Infantry. **1**: First version, 'pigeon-breasted' with oval base and white helmet (1899). **2** and **3**: Second version, 'pigeon-breasted' with square base and blue helmet (1908). A new larger head has been fitted. **4**: Fourth version 'closed elbow' (1928). **5**: Sailors at the slope, set 2080 (1954). **6**: Officers and petty officers, set 1911 (1940), which contained a selection of more modern officers in blue uniforms and white tropical kit. **7**: Sailors in regulation dress, set 1510 (1937). **8**: 'Eyes Right' Band of the Royal Marines, set H7283 (1961). **9**: Hill, No. 939, Royal Marine bugler (50mm 1925). **10**: Wellington Toy Company, Royal Marine Artillery (1910). **11**: Metasol, Royal Marine (1950). **12**: Lone Star, Harvey series, Royal Marine (1964). **13**: Britains, Royal Marine officer, fifth version, set 35 (1934). **14**: Britains, Royal Marine, sixth version, set 35 (1949). **15**: Blenheim, Royal Marine, set B 17 (S 1975). **16**: Blenheim, Band of the Royal Marines in capes, set H3 (S 1978). **17** and **18**: Marktime, naval landing-party and officer (S 1975). **19** and **20**: Imperialist, Nos. C10 and C12, Scroby-designed figures commissioned by the author (S 1976). **21–24**: Blenheim, Gatling gun and naval crew in sennet hats (S 1981). The Royal Navy with its Marines provided landing-parties to abet countless colonial skirmishes. Collectors today use many of these figures in their late nineteenth-century exhibits.

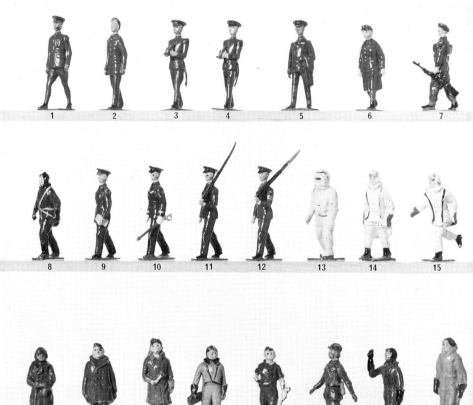

PLATE 40: ROYAL AIR FORCE (RAF)

1–13: Britains. **1**: RAF airman, peak cap, set 240 (1927). **2**: RAF display, airman in field cap, set 2011 (1948). **3**: RAF band, first version, set 1524 (1937). **4**: RAF band, second version with gold stripe down trousers, set 2116 (1955). **5**: Officer with coat over arm, set 2011 (1948), a repainting by Britains of a much earlier civilian figure, the yachtsman. **6**: Women's Auxiliary Air Force (WAAF), the same figure as **Plate 31**: 17 but in Air Force blue, set 1894 (1940). **7**: RAF Regiment with Bren-gun, set 2011 (1948). **8**: Pilot, set 1894 (1940). **9**: Set 2011 officer with clipboard. **10** and **11**: RAF at the slope, officer and airman, set 2073 (1953). **12**: RAF Colour-party, Colour Sergeant, set 2171 (1959). This was an extremely rare set. The only difference between **11** and **12** is the sergeant's silver stripes. **13**: Firefighter of the RAF, set 1758 (1939). **14** and **15**: Hill, pilots. Strictly speaking as these figures are in white flying-suits they are civilian pilots, the same figures being painted in khaki for the RAF. **16**: Hill, Pilot in long coat (1920). **17**: Hill, Airman in short coat (1920). **18**: Unknown (1930). **19**: Crescent, Pilot (1935). **20**: Hill, Mechanic with spanner (1920). **21**: Hill, WAAF (1939). **22**: Hill, Pilot (1948). **23**: Timpo, Pilot (60mm 1946), one of Timpo's very first products, made of composition material and often sold in sets with small-scale metal aircraft.

PLATE 41: BRITISH INDIA

1: Oojah-Cum-Pivvy, No. 022, Regimental Policeman, Pakistan Armoured Corps, 1983 (S 1983). **2**: Charbens (P 1964). **3**: Crescent (P 1964). These would appear to be using kukris, which are normally thought of as Gurkha knives. **4**: Hill (1920). **5**: Britains, Gurkha Rifles, the Malaun Regiment, set 197 (1916). **6**: Unknown, copy of **7** (1900), arm missing. **7–13**: Britains. **7** and **8**: 1st Madras Native Infantry, set 67 (1896), **8** being the pioneer included in early sets. These were Britains first infantry with movable arms. **9**: Special painting with rifle at the slope on the wrong shoulder, depicting 129th Baluch Regiment (1937). **10**: Special painting of the 12th Frontier Force, which also appeared as a standard set, No. 1621 (1938), using the same figure. **11–13**: Set 46, Hodson's Horse, earlier known as 10th Bengal Lancers. **11**: Trooper (1930). **12**: Trumpeter, usually included in single row sets (1896). **13**: Officer, usually included in double row set 63 (1896). **14**: Crescent, attractive figure of a lancer (1935). **15** and **16**: Britains, set 64, a double row set that included a set of 7th Bengal Infantry as well as these 2nd Madras Lancers (1896), later known as the 16th Light Cavalry when in the dark-blue jackets as **16** (1933). **17**: Heinrich, copy of a Britains 'rocking-horse' (1898). Although made in Germany, this figure is included here as an example of the only German firm to try hollow-casting on a scale competitive with Britains. Large quantities were exported to the UK 1898–1910.

57

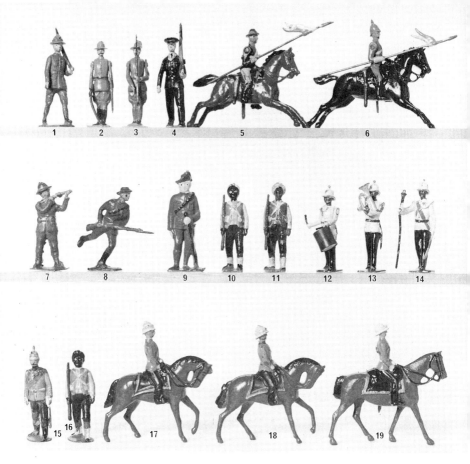

PLATE 42: BRITISH EMPIRE

1–6: Britains. **1**: New Zealand infantry, set 1542 (1937). **2**: New Zealand infantry at the present, officer, set 1543 (1937). **3**: Australian infantry at the present, set 1545 (1937), the only difference between **2** and **3** being in the hat. **4**: Australian infantry, blue pattern uniform, set 2030 (1949). **5** and **6**: Set 49, South Australian Lancers. **5**: First version, based on New South Wales Lancers before Queen Victoria's Diamond Jubilee (1896). **6**: Fourth version based on the Adelaide Lancers (1925). **7**: Reka, New Zealand infantry (1920), the end of the rifle is missing. **8**: Fry, Australian infantry (1916). **9**: Unknown, Australian infantry. **10**: Britains, West India Regiment, second version, set 19 (1932). **11**: Unknown, copy of **10** (1935). **12** and **14**: Britains, Bahamas Police Band, set 2186 (1959), a rare set sold only as a souvenir item in the Bahamas. The side drum provided for **12** is of plastic, and the transfer (decal) placed round it has flaked off, leaving the basic dark-blue. **15–19**: Britains, set 19, West India Regiment. **15**: Rare early 'bemedalled' officer on foot, indistinguishable from the first-version officer for set 18, Worcestershire Regiment. **16**: Normal West Indian with oval base, which was retained until 1932. **17–19**: Usually set 19 was provided with a mounted officer rather than one as **15**. **17**: Early variation with a curiously-shaped head. **18**: Normal officer until 1916. **19**: Normal officer 1920–40, although some later sets had no officer at all. The West India Regiment was Britains' first portrayal of colonial troops.

58

PLATE 43: BRITISH EMPIRE

1 and **2**: Britains, Australian infantry in battledress, set 2031 (1949). **1**: Officer. **2**: Private. This figure was made by providing the British infantry (see **Plate 34**: 1) with a new Australian head with slouch hat. **3**: Britains, Cape Town Highlanders, set 1901 (1940). **4**: Britains, Durban Light Infantry, set 1293 (1934), although it is normally necessary to possess the box in order to prove that it is this set rather than set 1294, British infantry in tropical dress. **5**: Britains, King's African Rifles, set 225 (1927). **6**: Halberd, Nigerian Regiment (1954). **7**: Britains, Royal Canadian Mounted Police in winter dress, set 214 (1924). **8**: Fry, Canadian infantry of the First World War (1915), this figure being painted in gold rather than khaki. **9**: Crescent, Royal Canadian Mounted Police (RCMP or Mountie) saluting (52mm 1948). **10** and **14**: Britains, RCMP mounted, set 1349 (1934). This figure was also used for US Cavalry in action, and the second version of the South African Mounted Infantry. **10**: Officer. **14**: Trooper. This figure was always provided with a long rifle rather than a carbine. **11**: Halberd, Mountie (1954). **12**: Hill, No. 918, Mountie (1925). **13**: Britains, Picture Pack No. 1373B, RCMP with lance (1954). This figure was only available singly, but since then Britains have produced similar figures in the 'Eyes Right' and New Metal ranges. **15**: Timpo, Mountie (1951). The rider can be dismounted from the horse. **16**: Unknown, Mountie (1950). **17**: Britains, No. 121P, RCMP (1951), second-grade figure. **18**: Hill, Mountie, set CP 18 (1925). This figure and **12** above were used in a number of different combination sets.

59

PLATE 44: EUROPE

Manufacturers other than Britains were not inclined to produce models of European armies. Only **4, 5** and **7–10** are not Britains. **1**: Prussian Hussar, set 153 (1908). **2**: Prussian Infantry, set 154 (1908). **3**: Austro-Hungarian Infantry of the Line, with red trousers, first version with long sword-bayonet visible behind the legs, set 177 (1913). **4**: Reka, Austrian (1913). **5**: BMC, Austrian (1913). **6**: Austro-Hungarian Foot Guard, second version, set 178 (1920). **7**: Fry, Austrian (1914), top of rifle missing. **8**: BMC, Serbian (60mm 1913). **9**: BMC, Italian Bersagliere (60mm 1911). The Britannia Model Company, despite its name, produced some excellent figures of foreign troops. **10**: Reka, Italian Bersagliere (1911). **11** and **12**: Set 169, Italian Bersagliere. **11**: First version (1912). **12**: Officer, added to the set much later (1954). **13** and **14**: Set 1437, Carabiniere, Italian police. **13**: Officer, added to the set later (1954). **14**: Second version, man (1954), the first version in 1937 had a red over dark-blue plume rather than red over light-blue as here. **15**: Admiral (see **Plate 38**: 8), repainted by Britains as a special Carabiniere officer (1939). **16**: Set 170, Greek Cavalry, one of the rarest Britains sets (1913). **17**: Greek Infantry, third 'closed elbow' version, set 171 (1928). **18**: Greek Evzones in red jacket, set 196 (1916). After 1946 the jacket was painted blue. **19**: Bulgarian Infantry officer, set 172 (1913). The cap is white with a light-blue line. **20**: Montenegrin infantry with red 'pillbox' cap, set 174 (1913). This assortment of East European troops was stimulated by the Balkan wars of the period. **21** and **22**: Turkish Infantry, set 167 (1911). The officer, **22**, is only found in sets until 1916, after which there were just eight men in the set.

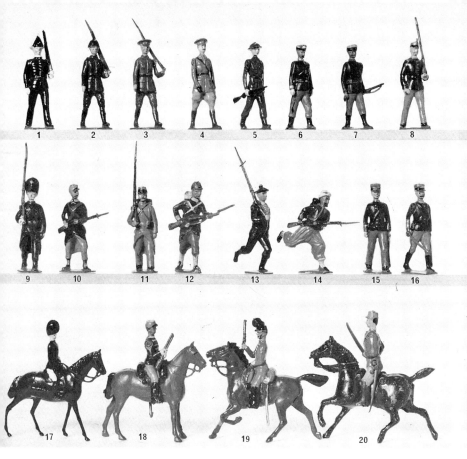

PLATE 45: EUROPE

All figures except **12** and **20** are Britains. **1**: Sweden, Svea Life Guard, set 2035 (1949). **2**: Polish Infantry, set 1856 (1939). The same figure in different colours was used for Netherlands and Argentine infantry, both extremely rare sets. **3–5**: Set 1603, Irish Free State (Eire) infantry. **3**: First version (1937). **4**: Officer, second version (1948), the moustache is an embellishment by a collector. **5**: Second-version, man (1948). This is an interesting combination of a US infantry body with a British head and arm. **6–8**: Set 92, Spanish infantry. **6**: First-version 'bemedalled' officer (1898). **7**: First-version man with 'valise pack' (1898). These are ordinary British Army figures adapted with new heads. **8**: Second version (1925), a specially designed figure. **9**: Belgian Grenadier, set 2009 (1948). **10**: Belgian infantry, set 189 (1915). **11**: French Infanterie de Ligne, set 141 (1905), first version with oval base. **12**: BMC, French infantry (1906). **13**: French matelot (sailor) first version with Lebel rifle at the slope, set 143 (1905). **14**: French Zouave, set 142 (1905). **15**: Officer to go with **14** (1905). This officer was adjudged not capable of keeping up with the charging Zouaves, and so was taken out of the set quite early on. From 1954 a mounted officer was included. **16**: This officer was sometimes included with sets of **11**, but more widely used by Britains' Paris branch (1909). **17**: No. 135P, Belgian Horse Gendarme (1952), a second-grade figure, the Scots Grey with appropriate colouring. **18**: Belgian Cavalry, set 190 (1915). **19**: French Chasseurs à Cheval, set 139 (1905). **20**: Unknown, French Hussar (1910).

PLATE 46: RUSSIA AND THE FAR EAST

1: Britains, Chinese infantry, set 241 (1927). These look more like irregulars, somewhat late for the Boxer uprising in 1900. 2: Imperialist, No. C3, Chinese green banner infantry with pike (1975). 3: Charbens, modern Chinese infantry (58mm P 1963). 4: Reka, Japanese infantry (1905). 5: Britains, Japanese Infantry in Fair paint condition, set 134 (1904). Some early sets of these had a different cap without a crown. 6: Unknown, most attractive figure of a Japanese soldier standing with grounded rifle (1905). 7 and 8: Bastion, Japanese Infantry 'New Toy Soldier' style (S 1982). This manufacturer has produced all the armies present at the siege of the Peking Legations in 1900, during the Boxer Uprising. 9: TAG, Cossack (70mm 1947), composition figure. 10: Crescent, Russian with submachine-gun (P 1964). 11: Britains, Russian Infantry, set 133 (1904). This figure is more usually found at the trail, but early sets had some at the slope included. 12 and 13: Timpo, Cossacks (P 1959). 14: Reka, Japanese Cavalry (1906). The horse is a copy of a Britains 'pony horse'. 15 and 17: BMC, Cossacks (1905), 15 has a brown overcoat, while 17 has a green coat and red trousers. The horse is the same for each. 16: Unknown, Cossack (1920). 18: Britains, Cossack, set 136 (1905). This was a most popular set, which continued in production until 1966. The great interest in Russian and Japanese troops was stimulated by the Russo-Japanese war of 1904–5.

PLATE 47: ARABS AND FRENCH FOREIGN LEGION

A favourite recent subject for children at play, so most manufacturers made a set during the 1950s. **1**: Britains, Bedouin Arabs marching, set 187 (1915). **2**: Unknown, copy of **1**, but with fixed arm (1920). **3**: Crescent, Arab (1930). **4**: Britains, Bedouin Arab mounted, set 164 (1911). **5**: Britains, Arabs, set 2046 (1950). **6**: Timpo, Arab (P 1976). **7**: Britains, Togoland Warrior, set 202 (1922). This subject admittedly originates from West Africa, somewhat south of the Sahara. **8**: Britains, Picture Pack, 1367B (1954), once a Paris Office figure (compare **Plate 45**: 15) now revived to lead the Legion. **9**: Britains, French Foreign Legion in action, set 2095 (1954). **10**: Trojan, Legionnaire (P 1960). **11**: Charbens, Legionnaire (P 1959). **12**: Timpo, Legionnaire to match **6** (P 1976). **13** and **14**: Britains Deetail, French Foreign Legion, set 7784 (P 1975). **15**: Crescent, No. A40, French Foreign Legion (1930), although the colour scheme with red jacket is more suggestive of British infantry at the time of the Indian Mutiny. **16**: Wend-Al, Legionnaire on camel (58mm A 1950). The aluminium casting process, using sand moulds, was imported from France, as were some master figures, including this one. **17**: Unknown, arab on camel (1925). **18**: Hill, arab on camel (1937). **19**: Britains, arabs of the desert on camels, set 193 (1916). This figure could lay claim to being the most magnificent model ever made by Britains. From the date of issue one might suppose that they were due to the exploits of Lawrence of Arabia, except that early boxes are marked 'Types of the Enemy'.

PLATE 48: UNITED STATES OF AMERICA (USA)

All the figures are Britains. **1–4** and **6**: set 91, United States infantry in blue uniform. **1**: Early variation with full dress infantry helmet (1898). **2**: Normal first-version 'valise pack' figure in Montana hat (1898). **3**: 'Bemedalled' officer to go with **2** (1898). **4**: Second-version figure (1906). **5**: The same figure as **4**, but coloured khaki as a special painting (1934). **6**: Second-version officer (1906). **7** and **8**: Set 1251, US infantry firing. **7**: Rare first version based, as were the standing and lying figures, on ordinary British Army figures in gaiters with a campaign hat added (1933). **8**: Second version, the same figure reworked with correct puttees (1934). **9**: US infantry, service dress (doughboy) in campaign hat, set 227 (1927). **10**: The same set, late variation with steel helmet (1940). Until 1942 the US Army used the same flat Mark I helmet as the British Army. Both armies then designed their own more protective successor, but owing to the shortage of steel the British Mark III was only partially introduced by the end of the war. In 1940–41, Britains could convert numerous sets into steel helmets and export them to the USA as US Army figures. **11**: Officer, set 227 (1927). **12**: US infantry, set 2033 (1949). **13**: Picture Pack, 1206B (1954). **14**: US Military Police, nicknamed 'Snowdrops' from their white helmets, set 2021 (1948). This set introduced the new US helmet to the Britains range. **15** and **16**: Band of the US Army in steel helmets, set 2117 (1955). **17**: US Cavalry, Service Dress, set 229 (1927). **18**: Bluejackets, set 230 (1927). **19**: Set 1253, Whitejackets, officer, included in later sets (1946). **20**: US Marines, sergeant, set 228 (1927). **21**: US Marines, active service order, set 399 (1929). **22**: Cavalryman in steel helmet (1940).

PLATE 49: USA AND LATIN AMERICA

It is curious that Britains only provided models of military cadets for the New World, a number of which are shown here. All figures are Britains except **17–19**. **1**: Mexican Infantry, set 186 (1915). **2**: Venezuela, military school cadets, set 2098 (1955). **3**: West Point cadets, winter dress, set 226 (1927). **4**: West Point cadets, summer dress, set 299 (1929). **5**: US infantry, small size, set 158W (45mm 1932), second-grade paint). **6** and **7**: Types of US Cavalry, small size (45mm 1932) second-grade paint. **8**: Argentine cadet, military school, set 219 (1925). **9**: Argentine infantry, set 216 (1925). **10**: Uruguayan infantry, set 222 (1925). **11**: Uruguayan cadet, military school, set 221 (1925). **8–11** were excellent models, each individually moulded for their subject. **12**: Uruguay, military school cadet, set 2051 (1954), a completely different figure from **11**. **13**: Argentine naval cadet, set 1835 (1939). **14**: Argentine military school cadet, set 1836 (1939). **15**: Argentine infantry, steel helmets, set 1837 (1939). Sets **13–15** were not widely distributed, and thus are rare. **16**: Argentine cavalry, set 217 (1925), here shown in 1950s paint style. The Uruguayan cavalry are very similar, but with the top of the shako dark-blue rather than yellow. **17–19**: Timpo, US Army, set 917 (1952). **20**: Set 276, US Cavalry in action, the original figure from which the more widely distributed RCMP set was derived (see **Plate 43**: 10 and 14).

PLATE 50: USA HISTORICAL

1: Britains, 'Eyes Right' American infantry, War of Independence, set 7384 (1965). **2**: Timpo, model of the same war, British redcoat (1963). **3**: Hill, US Whitejacket (1950). **4** and **5** and **7–20**: West Point cadets in their early 19th century uniform, a favourite subject in the USA, and thus good for British export. **4** and **5**: Hill, two versions (1950 and 1954). **6**: Hill, US Marine (1954). **7–20**: Timpo, a series which was started as a wide range in metal, and was then remoulded in plastic with almost identical designs, the plastic figures, **8, 10** and **15** (P 1958), being slightly smaller. Compare **8** with **16**, the metal equivalent. There were twenty different figures in the metal series (1952), a larger series of military master models than anything produced for one group by Britains. There were eleven boxed sets on the market, as well as the models being sold individually. The largest set, No. 790, was a two-tier set containing the band and marching figures, forty-eight in all. The firing figures were in set 731, and the drill positions in set 750. **21**: Timpo, Confederate (P 1957). **22** and **23**: Lone Star, Harvey Series, Confederates. **22** was a re-colouring of a Foreign Legion figure with kepi (P 1958), while **23** shows the same figure properly converted by Lone Star to a confederate with a cut down kepi and shorter coat (P 1959). **24**: Blenheim, Union infantry, an experimental figure repainted by Blenheim from the casting used for set B39, South Carolina Volunteers (S 1977).

PLATE 51: USA HISTORICAL

The American Civil War received no attention at all from British toy manufacturers until 1951, when Britains brought out a series in metal, primarily as an export line. From then on there has been at least one series in Britains range, and many other firms followed suit. 1–3: Britains, complete set 2141, Confederate cavalry (1957), one of the half-size boxes produced only from 1957 to 1959. 4: Britains, set 2059, Confederate infantry, this figure on guard having a 'butternut' brown jacket (1951). 5: Britains, Picture Pack, 1362B (1954). This is the same as the French Zouave with the addition of a gold stripe down the trouser. 6: Britains, Union infantry, standard-bearer, set 2059 (1951). All seven of the figures in the infantry set were different. 7 and 8: Charbens, Confederates (P 1962). 9 and 10: Charbens (P 1970), a later series with 'Swoppet'-style parts. 11: Timpo, Union infantry (P 1957). 12: Timpo, 7th Cavalry (P 1970). This historically depicts the era just after the Civil War, when Custer was fighting the Sioux. The convention among toy soldier makers was to show these troops wearing braces. 9 and 10 have moulded braces, but are produced in Confederate grey plastic, thus letting the moulds do duty for two roles. 13: Britains, Picture Pack, 1360B, Union cavalry at the halt, rather than trotting as in the normal set (1954). 14: Britains, 'Eyes Right' No. 450, Union officer (P 1962). 15 and 16: Britains, Deetail series 7449, Federal cavalry (1972).

67

PLATE 52: MEDIEVAL

Knights in armour have in latter years provided subjects for many popular toys, especially since the popularity of Robin Hood and other historical costume dramas in film and on television. **1** and **2**: Courtenay and Doran (45mm 1930). **3**: Cherilea, bowman (50mm 1952). **4**: Cherilea, crossbowman from their Robin Hood series (48mm P 1957), this example has been repainted. **5** and **6**: Herald, Swoppets, 15th-century Knights, Wars of the Roses series (P 1959). These are some of the most elegant archers ever made – **6** is a crossbowman. **7**: Lone Star, Harvey Series, Sheriff of Nottingham with a problem (P 1959). **8**: Lone Star, man-at-arms (P 1959). While most firms produced knights, the men-at-arms and archers were not so often made. **9–12**: Cherilea. **9**: Saracen emblem-bearer (50mm 1953). Many collectors think of these figures more as Assyrians than Saracens, but they were sold to oppose **10** and **11**: Crusaders (50mm 1951). **12**: Knight on foot, set S/306 (50mm 1951). **13**: Crescent, mounted knight (1950). **14** and **15**: Hill, set 48/82 (1904), some of the earliest and most widely distributed knights in armour. **16**: Cherilea, superb model of King Richard I (1953). This firm made a feature of their character figures, which included one of the Duke of Marlborough. **17**: Cherilea, knight, set S/307 (1951). **18** and **19**: Timpo, character figures made to go with the MGM film *Quentin Durward* (1956). **18**: No. HF 500, Quentin Durward himself. **19**: No. HF 501, the arch-villain, Philip de Creville (see also **Plate 53**: 8). The hands of these figures are shaped to take the hilts of separate metal swords, usually missing as here.

PLATE 53: MEDIEVAL

1–3: Benbros, Robin Hood series (1954). **1**: Much the Miller's son. **2**: The Bishop of Hereford. **3**: Sheriff of Nottingham's guard. **4**: Charbens (1949). **5–8**: Timpo. **5**: Crusader hiding behind his shield (P 1960). **6**: Knight (P 1970). **7**: First series knight in plastic (P 1958). **8**: No. HF 510, Quentin Durward series, Royal Guard (1956). The hand is shaped to hold a plastic spear (see also **Plate 52**: 18 and 19). **9**: Sacul (1953), with movable lance arm. The two knobs on the helmet are to hold a movable visor which is missing. **10**: Lone Star, Harvey series (P 1957). **11**: Lone Star, 'Metallion', King Arthur, from the Knights of the Round Table series (56mm D 1976). These figures were distributed unpainted in a metallic finish. **12**: Timpo (1952), holding a wire and solder spear. **13**: Britains, 16th-century knight, set 1307 (1934). **14** and **15**: Britains, Medieval tournament, set 1258 (1933). **14**: Herald. **15**: Tournament Marshal. **16**: Timpo, Crusader, a figure originally made for the MGM film *Ivanhoe*, but then produced as a series of crusaders in four different colours (1955), the lance is plastic. **17**: Timpo, KN 57, Sir Hugh de Bracy from the Ivanhoe series (1954) with cast metal lance. **18**: Herald, No. H1453, Swoppet 15th-century Knight, Wars of the Roses series (P 1960). A multitude of different plug-in crests, visors and shields were made, offering millions of different Swoppet combinations. **19**: Timpo, a late-series knight (P 1972). The feature of the series was the flamboyant heraldic stickers for the banners and shields.

PLATE 54: HISTORICAL – ANCIENT WORLD

1: Herald, Trojan Warriors, set 7590 (P 1956). This series was dropped from the catalogue after 1962, but revived in 1966 as a series made in Hong Kong, as shown here. **2–6**: Cherilea, Egyptians and Nubians series (P 1963). **2**: Sphinx. **3**: Nubian air-conditioning engineer. **4**: Character figure of Cleopatra. **5**: Nubian slave with genuine metal chain. **6**: Egyptian archer. **7–13**: Romans. **7**: Kew (1924). **8**: Hill, No. 569A, Roman gladiator (1922). **9**: Marx, of brittle plastic, produced in Hong Kong, particularly for the British market (60mm P 1965). **10** and **11**: Crescent, Gladiators series (P 1959), these figures have been repainted by the author. At this time Crescent figures were all produced on large rectangular bases, and coded underneath. These two are coded RG (Roman Gladiator) 3 and RG 2. **12** and **13**: Timpo (P 1967), an attractive series of figures with interchangeable legs and torsos, and removable shields and weapons. At this time Timpo were developing a method of pouring more than one colour of plastic into a mould to replace hand painting, a technology also used more recently by Britains. **14** and **15**: Reynolds, Vikings (1953). **16**: Benbros, Greek chariot (D 1950). **17**: Timpo, Viking (P 1974), one of the last series made by Timpo. Four colours of plastic have been poured and bonded to make this lovely figure, which has no hand painting on it. **18–20**: Cherilea (60mm P 1961). **18**: Viking. **19**: Ancient Briton. **20**: Boudicea, who also came with a plug to fit on to a chariot. The pattern of production of these plastic historical series tended to be six different figures depicting each subject.

PLATE 55: HISTORICAL – 16TH CENTURY ONWARDS

1 and **2**: Cherilea, 16th-century soldiers (P 1964). These moulds were taken over from a previous manufacturer, possibly Monarch, in a move common among toy soldier manufacturers when firms ran into difficulties. **3** and **4**: Cherilea, 16th-century figures (60mm P 1961). **5** and **6**: Two figures originated by the Swedish sculptor Holger Eriksson. **5**: Swedish African Engineers (SAE), Swedish dragoon of the 17th century, made in South Africa (S 1956). **6**: Malleable Mouldings, version of the same subject (P 1948). **7**: Cherilea, another 16th-century figure (60mm P 1961). **8**: Britain's No. T-1 character figure of Henry VIII made especially for Madame Tussaud's waxworks museum souvenir shop (67mm 1935). **9**: Courtenay, executioner, to accompany Mary Queen of Scots (S 1955). Courtenay figures are almost models in quality, but still have much of the toy about them, since he started his modelling career as a toy maker (see **Plate 54**: 1 and 2). **10** and **11**: Herald, set H7402, Roundheads and Cavaliers. These are the two mounted figures from the series of six (P 1958). These superb figures of the English Civil War are acclaimed as some of the finest toy soldiers ever produced. **12**: Charbens, 18th-century Fusilier (P 1959). **13**: Blenheim, set B2, Coldstream Guards at Waterloo (S 1975). **14**: Benbros, Waterloo infantry (1951). **15**: Britains, line infantry, Waterloo period, carrying pike, set 1516 (1937), showing the early paint variation with blue rather than grey trousers. **16–18**: Timpo, Waterloo series (P 1959). **16** and **17**: British Infantry. **18**: French Dragoon. The series comprised four mounted figures and eight infantry figures for each of the three major participants in the battle, French, British and Prussians. **19**: Britains, Deetail No. 7959, French cavalry at Waterloo series, French Cuirassier (P 1974).

71

INDEX BY MANUFACTURER

*Dates refer to the approximate period during which
toy soldiers were manufactured.*